An Illustrated History
of

THE ISLE OF WIGHT RAILWAYS
Cowes to Newport

By Oliver Smith

For Syd

Copyright Irwell Press 1993
ISBN 1-871608-32-5
Printed by Amadeus Press, Huddersfield
First published in United Kingdom by Irwell Press,
15 Lovers Lane,
Grasscroft,
OLDHAM OL4 4DP

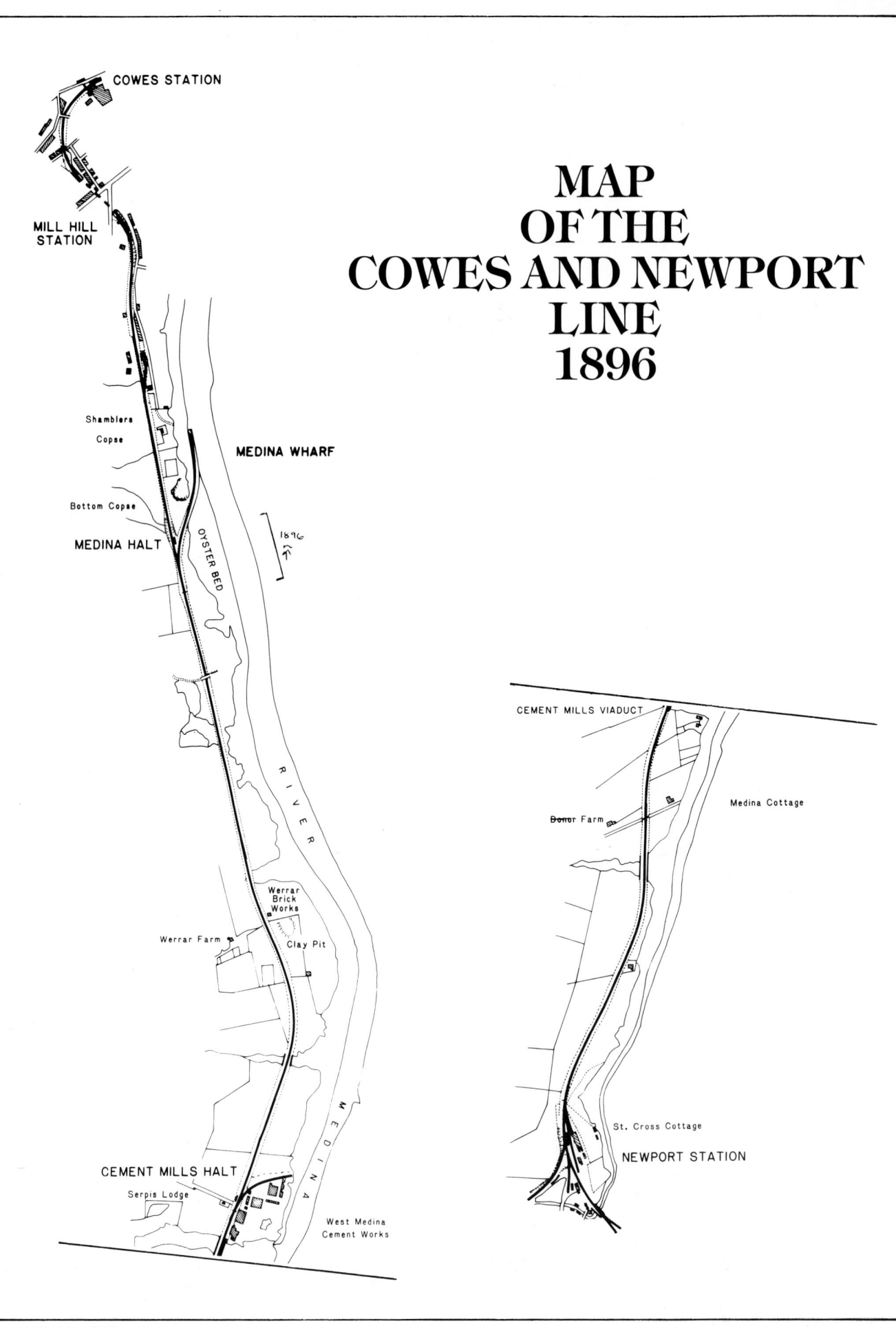

INTRODUCTION
'A Most Noisy and very Rowdy Meeting'

So much has been said derogatory to the interests of the Isle of Wight Railways that it behoves one actively engaged in their management to seek to enlist public sympathy on their behalf in view of the extenuating circumstances not apparent to the casual observer, for such imperfections as do exist.

Thus spoke C.L. Conacher, of the Isle of Wight Central Railway, a man of whom we shall hear more anon. The multifarious nature of railways in the Isle of Wight is matched only by the range of descriptions available for those wishing to acquaint themselves with the islands' fascinating railway past. It is a complex story, in miniature a reflection of the epic struggle and rivalries of the mainland giants. The Isle of Wight railways have indeed attracted considerable attention, due, amongst a wealth of factors, to convenient geographical limitations and the charm of a wholly unique setting.

There has long been an air about the Isle of Wight, diminished now by changing taste and fashion almost to vanishing point. Indeed, much that was best about 'rural England' seemed encapsulated in the Island to a singular degree. This has impressed itself upon numbers of writers, jostling one another to praise the island paradise: *England in Cameo*, *England's Eden* are nineteenth and early twentieth century descriptions that still hold true, in part, and captivating scenery awaits those willing to wander the byways. Windswept chalk downland ('beloved of Tennyson') contrasts with rich clay pastureland, sheltered mudflats with broken rocky cliffs. The island can delight the antiquarian, the naturalist, the geologist and, still even today, the railway enthusiast; there remain many features of railway interest on the island, though they continue a slow waning and are but sad echoes of what once was. Into the late 'fifties and even the 'sixties the locomotives and rolling stock had an ancient look, things wholly singular to the island, and journeys by train were still as much part of the island's way of life as the ferry trip to the mainland.

Railways in the Isle of Wight were somehow quintessentially *English*; along with much that was good they survived the Second World conflict only to perish in the blinkered period that followed. As early as 1950 certain of the islands' railways were already regarded as anachronisms, well into the autumn of their years. With winter fast approaching they were locked into the past, the optimism and expansion of the Southern Railway era, which attained a peak in the 1930s, gone forever. The first closure came in the early 1950s, accompanied by a lasting bitterness and rancour, undiminished when the rest of the system all but expired in 1966, the year The Plot ripened.

What then of the lines themselves? The Isle of Wight Central Railway, though not the most financially secure, grew from a bewildering collection of companies, with four routes centred on Newport. Its nucleus had been the Cowes and Newport Railway, opened in 1862 and the Ryde and Newport Railway, connec-

Archetypal scene at Cowes. The station, perched awkwardly on a hillside, was erected in a district characterised by mean dwellings and accordingly held in low esteem; it could never, unfortunately, claim to be much above its surrounds in this regard. The station was much rebuilt and expanded over the years, the work accomplished in several episodes, with extension of the platforms and enlargement of the buildings. Clearances associated with (perhaps under the cloak of) this work eliminated the 'most noxious' of the dwellings round about but the district was never considered salubrious.

ting the island's major holiday resort with the County Town in 1875. The latter was worked "as an integral part of the Cowes and Newport Railway system, the management being vested in a Joint Committee of the two Boards". The grandly titled 'Isle of Wight (Newport Junction) Railway', (usually called simply the Newport Junction Railway) subsequently inched its way painfully from Sandown, finally reaching Newport in 1879, only to fall into receivership in 1880. It was afterwards administered by the Joint Committee at Newport, and all three companies were amalgamated as the 'Isle of Wight Central Railway' in 1887. The independent Freshwater, Yarmouth and Newport Railway opened shortly afterwards, to be worked by the IWCR and in 1897 another over-optimistic venture, the Newport, Godshill and St. Lawrence Railway, opened from Merstone on the Newport Junction Line. It was extended to Ventnor Town in 1900 and absorbed by the Central, which had always worked it, in 1913. The Freshwater company retained a measure of independence asserted (as far as the IWCR was concerned) with a tiresome regularity. It proved a troublesome neighbour more or less throughout its existence, until all the island lines were joined with the Southern Railway under the 1923 Grouping. The Freshwater Company was an almost compulsive litigant – it opened for goods in 1888 and passengers the following year, taking over its own services from the Isle of Wight Central, and putting up its own station, in July 1913. This was the culmination of years of legal tussle and the minute company even held out against Grouping, disputing terms with the Southern until formal absorption in August 1923. The remaining island company (leaving aside the pier at Ryde) was a rival which for years the Central could hardly bring itself to even acknowledge, though it outlived all the other concerns and survives in truncated, electrified, form even today. The Isle of Wight Railway opened from Ryde to Shanklin in 1864 and was completed through to Ventnor two years later. A branch to Bembridge followed in 1882.

The civic-minded noble, Lord Yarborough, is largely credited with seeing off an 1845 proposal for a railway to Cowes, landed interests manifesting then and subsequently a considerable hostility. A meeting at Newport on 14th December 1852 to present another scheme, the 'Isle of Wight Railway' for connecting Newport, Ryde, Cowes and Ventnor 'in one continuous line' was abandoned more or less in disarray, or worse. Landowners inevitably opposed the scheme and had enlisted support from certain vital Newport interests (at no time could the town ever have been said to have viewed the railway with other than indifference). The editor of the *Hampshire Advertiser* spoke of the line's promoters in the following terms: "We have only space to express our disgust at the unwarrantable

0–4–4T No.28 ASHEY at Cowes on the 11.28am to Ryde on 7th August 1965. Map evidence shows the station fronting 'Carvel Lane' from the earliest days though one side street at least served for access, the unpromisingly named Hog Lane. "At last after many delays" the line opened on 21st June 1862, "first trains having run on Monday morning. Those who have ridden over the line think it is very pleasant travelling. Certainly it is quick as the journey lasts but 10 minutes. The fares are thought by many to be rather high, as many of the labouring classes passing between the towns would be glad to avail themselves were there 3rd Class fares". Passengers, it appeared, were "as numerous as would be expected". Photograph Leslie Sandler.

The modest Cowes signalbox. By 1875 (some three years since the Cowes and Newport had arrived at a formal working agreement with the Ryde and Newport) thought was given to further improvements at Cowes. It still had only a single line of rails after all and in June it was resolved to open negotiations for the purchase of land 'for improvement to the station and approaches'. At the end of the year £4,330 was made over to Martin for land and property 'adjoining and opposite Cowes station, to enable the proposed extensions to premises to be made'.

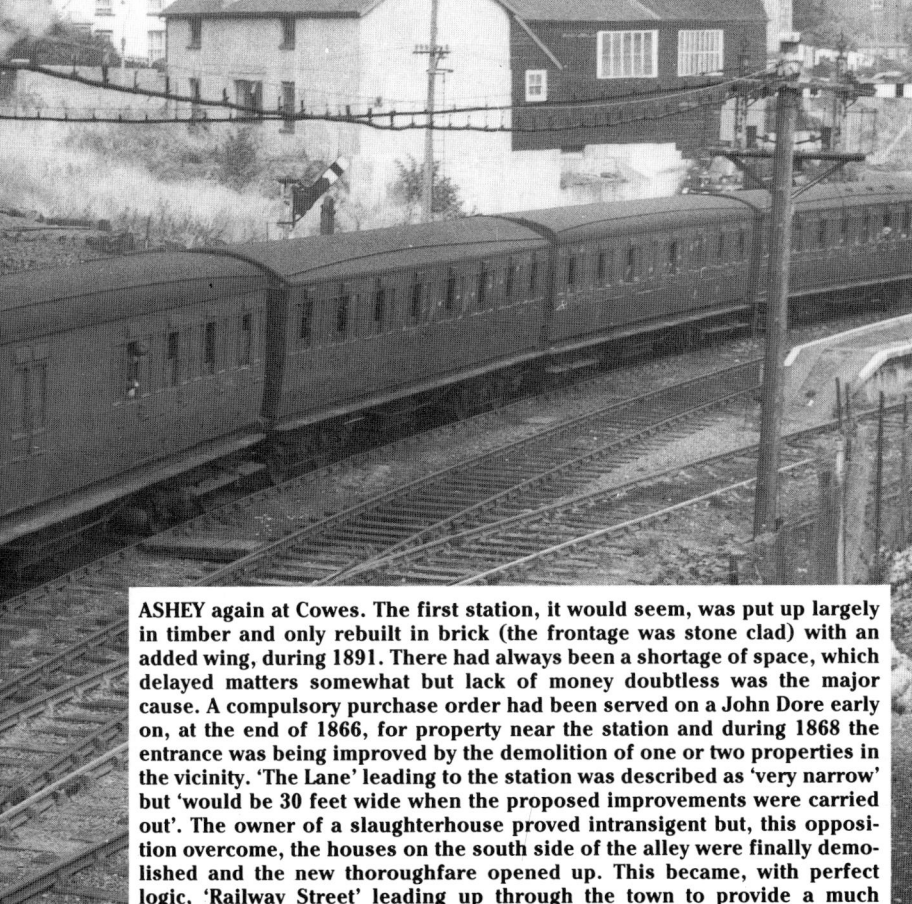

ASHEY again at Cowes. The first station, it would seem, was put up largely in timber and only rebuilt in brick (the frontage was stone clad) with an added wing, during 1891. There had always been a shortage of space, which delayed matters somewhat but lack of money doubtless was the major cause. A compulsory purchase order had been served on a John Dore early on, at the end of 1866, for property near the station and during 1868 the entrance was being improved by the demolition of one or two properties in the vicinity. 'The Lane' leading to the station was described as 'very narrow' but 'would be 30 feet wide when the proposed improvements were carried out'. The owner of a slaughterhouse proved intransigent but, this opposition overcome, the houses on the south side of the alley were finally demolished and the new thoroughfare opened up. This became, with perfect logic, 'Railway Street' leading up through the town to provide a much improved approach to the station.

language used in speaking of the landed gentry of the island. It would be a perversion of terms to allow the proceedings of such a meeting to go forth as the voice of the town". The meeting succeeded nevertheless in appointing a local committee, its aim to assist in the securing of an Act and of this the *Advertiser* commented; "thus concluded one of the most successful and disreputable attempts to gag free dissension and to put down free discussion". This 'most noisy and very rowdy meeting' ended then on a note of some optimism for the proponents of an island railway.

Another, simultaneous, meeting was held at Cowes, expressing great support for the railway and Lord Yarborough's 1845 opposition, which had greatly swayed opinion in the town, was much regretted. Similar gatherings occurred at Ryde and Ventnor.

The Cowes and Newport Railway was a modest scheme, a little-regarded project enduring whilst more grandiose proposals, hatched in the 1850s, fizzled out. There was 'Birkenshaw's Railway' lauded in the local press and planned to join Cowes, Newport, Ryde, Sandown, Shanklin and Ventnor and others; 'Fulton's Scheme', that of 'Livesay and Saunders' and others. The Cowes and Newport Railway prospectus was issued as 1858 came to a close, several years after the heated Newport meeting and a manifestation of the islands' own unlikely *Railway Mania*.

The Directors of the Cowes and Newport Railway first met, in their official capacity at least, on 17th August 1859, at the *Fountain Hotel*, Cowes, under the chairmanship of H.W. Petre. This group of four worthies (as well as Mr Petre there was Henry Pinnock, later of the Ryde and Newport Railway Board, W.C. Hoffmeister of Cowes and R. Jewell of Newport) set briskly about the ordering of their railway. Costs were estimated at £34,000, the two stations, Cowes and Newport, were determined upon and the first compensations (the most, £415, to a Mr. Wheeler for passing through his mealyard) agreed. Contractor was a Mr. Fernandez, later to be replaced by Messrs. Jackson and White. By autumn surveyors were busy, even taking levels 'with a view to extending the Cowes and Newport onto Ventnor' – to go beyond Newport was the intention from the first. On 1st October the *Isle of Wight Observer* reported 'Work on the Cowes – Newport Section is to start at once'. The first sod, it was later to recount, was unostentatiously dug … 'on 16th October 1859'. This was a Sunday and *The Hampshire Independent* of 22nd October 1859 is probably more correct in its own account of the ceremonies at Cowes: 'At noon on 15th October (a Saturday) the first sod was turned in most unfavourable weather conditions, the rain scarcely ceasing all day . (Nevertheless) a considerable company assembled'. Neither Petre nor Ward (of the island's land owning family) could manage the necessary effort, through illness, but a well known local yacht-builder, Michael Ratsey ... 'proved an excellent substitute and wielded the barrow and shovel with a will'. After this he gave a brief speech followed by 'excellent champagne' upon which the party of 30 or so adjourned to *The Fountain* to be entertained by the contractor Mr. Fernandez'.

The spot (later to be the site of Mill Hill station) where work had been commenced was in the south east corner of a field lying between the Newport Road and 'the garden and reservoir of Messrs. White in the upper part of which field just beyond the house of Mr. Bannister the rope maker, the tunnel will be begun'. There was, as we have already noted, every intention to extend swiftly onto Ventnor, an expectation which, alas, was many years in the realising... *"To our great surprise the projectors of the Cowes and Newport Extension to Ventnor have not profited by the experience of last year when their Bill was thrown out through non-compliance with Standing Orders, especially with regard to errors in levels and on Wednesday last they again suffered defeat from the same cause. This, to say the least of it, implies bungling on the part of the engineers and the effect of it will be no doubt very vexatious to the friends of the scheme"*.

Work was 'still advancing' on the Cowes and Newport section in May 1861 when it was 'hoped to have the line ready for opening this year'. By September progress was still being made 'but not as quickly as hoped' and by October 'it was hoped' (again) to have the line 'ready for opening in a few weeks'. This was somewhat misplaced optimism, explained no doubt by the eagerness of anticipation felt by both builders and public. The island's first passenger line eventually opened the next year, to some considerable rejoicing – its novelty alone surety of success. Intolerant of delay the *Isle of Wight Observer* 'previewed' the line in November 1861.

Isle of Wight Observer, 2nd November 1861.

This railway commences at Cowes and its station is situated in Carvel Lane; and being several feet above the level of the street is reached by a flight of about twenty stairs. The station, as yet incomplete, has a general waiting room, departments for station master, etc. and for about 50 feet up the line is covered in. There is but one line of rails laid down and on leaving the station it forms a gentle curve until Mill Hill is reached under which there is a tunnel. As soon as the southern extremity is reached a view opens up of the River Medina and the line pursues its course by its side until Newport is reached, passing in succession the Cowes Gasworks, brickyard, through another brickyard, past the Cement Mills and then across a wooden viaduct about 100 feet in length, supported on wood piles erected over a small arm of the river. There are several bridges over the line and the most conspicuous objects visible from the line are the tower of St. Thomas's Church, the keep of Caris-

22 BRADING after arrival at Cowes (platform 2) with the 10.18 relief ex–Ryde St. John's Road, summer 1964. Photograph T.P. Cooper.

Below. Old No.1, the 2–2–2T originally named PIONEER, it played its part with PRECURSOR in the actual construction of the line and the years saw the names removed (straight plates on the boiler side) and something like an adequate cab, as well as detail alterations.

Above. A wooden engine shed and carriage shed had been provided at Cowes from the first, in style primitive enough to match the terminus. From July 1862 the first tenders were invited for 'Best Welsh Steam Coal' 20 tons a week delivered to the terminus at Cowes for PIONEER and PRECURSOR. Repairs to both locomotives and stock were carried out here, a daily miracle of improvisation. Once the Isle of Wight Central had been set up (officially the week ending Friday 1st July 1887) it was obvious that operations would be centred on Newport and as early as 27th September a letter to the Board of Directors outlined plans 'for removal of part of the shops'. All was delayed until the general rearrangements at Cowes in 1891 and in October 1890 a separate estimate was ordered 'for removal of the workshops and sheds to Newport'. There is a note at the end of the year, presumably referring to Newport; 'Purchase of land from Winchester College completed, December 1890.' After the transfer of repair work to Newport there is reference to 'finishing off' the Cowes station ('three iron buffer stops', £23 each). In it Herbert Simmons, the General Manager, referred to 'the necessity for an Engine Pit at Cowes.' It does not seem to have been provided. This remarkable photograph, from 1876, comes to us through a singular and alarming episode in the history of Cowes. It was immortalised by the press in the autumn of 1876 – *Cowes Devastated by Tornado, The Whirlwind at Cowes* and so on. The minutes of the Cowes and Newport Railway are characteristically silent on the matter but the *Chronicle* among others refers to Cowes carriage shed damaged and carriages blown over. According to *The Graphic* of 7th October 1876 the first indication was 'an unwanted heaviness in the atmosphere and the appearance of a great number of birds flying about as if in alarm.' The violent wind lasted only a few seconds and did not extend more than about 100 feet in width but in that short time and in that limited area it accomplished 'an amount of destruction almost incredible.' Something, at least, remained of Cowes 'shops' – most probably the engine shed rehabilitated for some other local purpose, until at least the turn of the century. In November 1903 under the heading 'Cowes Station and Works' the Directors recorded an offer of £1 per month 'for rent of vacant premises' from a Mr. Bevan. The Directors were nothing it not businessmen and retorted that they 'could not accept an offer less than £2'.

Plan, Cowes, 1862

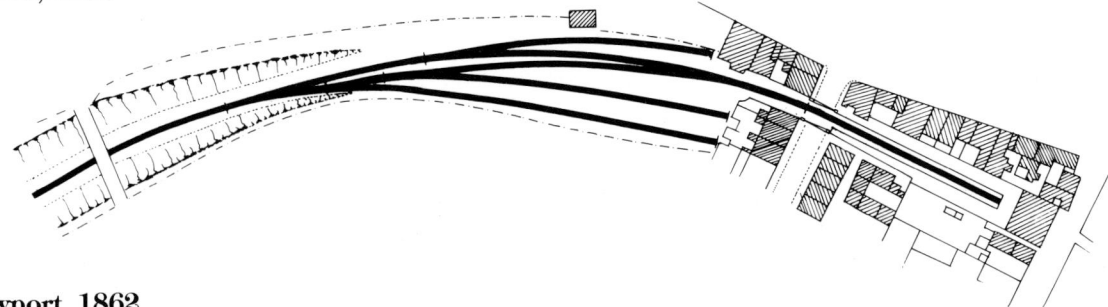

Plan, Newport, 1862

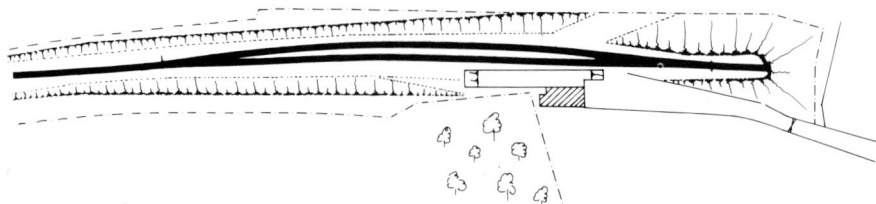

brook Castle, Parkhurst Barracks and Prison, the Poor House, the downs above Newport and the green and shubberied banks of the River Medina. The rails are laid down nearly the whole length of the line except for about ½ mile near Newport. A large number of navvies are employed on the works. The Newport termination of the line is close to Woodwar Wharf, Sea Street, but no station accommodation is yet erected there. The engines have arrived at Cowes and have already run up and down the completed part of the line for test etc. and the carriages are on the road; so the opening of

Southern Railway 0-4-4T No.32 BONCHURCH at Newport. The island lines were operated by a succession of tank engines and stock which whilst adequate for the needs of the Eden Isle, could never elude that air of quaintness – not that anyone particularly desired it otherwise – except of course Conacher. He sought to escape this enforced parochiality, pitching for a national setting for his 'Central' His classic *apologia, Multum in Parvo* in *The Railway Magazine* of 1899 put the Isle of Wight's case by exhaustively (and misleadingly) relating it to other companies: "Dealing first with the passenger traffic, the following comparison will serve to show that my title is not misapplied in this respect. In 1897 no fewer than 1,500,000 persons were conveyed on the island lines upon a train mileage of 318,000 miles, whereas on the Hull and Barnsley railway, 77 miles in length, and connecting populous centres, practically a fourth of that number only were carried". Charles ignored of course the vast mineral traffic of the H&B, the main purpose to which its construction had been devoted in the first place. Yorkshire concern with the everyday and pressing task of wresting an income from its dour activities doubtless meant that little if any reaction to this 'damned statistics' stuff was ever forthcoming.
Left. Newport shed, with its curiously, unconventionally, sited water tank, 3rd November 1956. Photograph A.E. Bennett.

9F. Old Southern No.8, an Isle of Wight Central 2–4–0T, at Newport, works buildings beyond and shed (with water tank – see opposite) to the right. In Conacher the IWCR had a spokesman who addressed his calling with an enthusiasm approaching the excessive, one suspects. He went on to give a series of examples justifying the 'Central's case, from the Cambrian to the Midland Great Western of Ireland – neither of them, incidentally, noted for any particular commercial galvanism. Compared to the 56 miles of island lines, apparently, with their 1½ million passengers the Cambrian (for whom Conacher would later – unsuccessfully – work) could boast 'only 720,000 more people, on 250 miles of line' whilst the latter, 'a still more striking example' despite possessing 'ten times the mileage' managed to convey nearly ¼ million less passengers…

Conacher raised the concept of 'putting on a gloss' to unheard 0f heights and from here, Newport, the heart of his empire, he held forth. From the laborious examples above, he attested (beginning to believe his own publicity it would seem): 'The Isle of Wight Railways play no mean part in the passenger traffic of the country and, indeed, are in the van for the high rate of earning per mile of line…'

the line may be expected very shortly to take place.

The contractors until this time had relied entirely on horses, for it was not until 5th October 1861 that the *Hampshire Advertiser* recorded "the first engines have commenced running on the Cowes and Newport line though at present they are only employed with ballast wagons. Being the first engines in the Isle of Wight they are a novelty and hundreds run to see them". *The Hampshire Independent* of the same day noted "the first steam engine for the Cowes and Newport has for some days past been running along that line between the terminus and Medham to test the road. The Government Inspector will make his visit very shortly." By the end of October 1861 the works were said to be 'approaching Newport' with a wooden bridge under way at the end of Holyrood Street to connect the station with the town. At the time the north end of Holyrood Street was blocked by a building labelled 'County Police and Bridewell'. Passengers descended a narrow passage at the side of this and across the wooden bridge (over the Lukely Brook) to reach the station.

Meeting again at the *Fountain Hotel* in February 1862, the Board noted that despite the financial failure of Fernandez, the works were 'being pushed on speedily'. Rolling stock, much of it stored in the open at Cowes, was awaiting the great day, delayed largely due to trouble with landslips. Henry Daniel Martin was engineer for the line and reported much of the plant 'in place'; he reckoned the trip Cowes – Newport would take some eleven minutes – 'coaches at present taking nearly an hour'. A station at Dodnor for Parkhurst was discussed and discounted; 'Mr. Bird questions the desirability of stopping the trains at Parkhurst by signal or otherwise'. One at least of the shareholders thought it a useful idea 'but it was decided to defer the matter pending opening of the line.' There is no written record of Dodnor station but even until recent times remains of a platform of sorts were visible.

On Saturday afternoon, 3rd May 1862, the 'first experimental train' was run 'consisting of engine, tender' [obviously purely a temporary arrangement during the contract period] 'and a carriage filled with workmen' from Cowes to Newport. The report of the *Isle of Wight Observer* notes the 'curiosity among the dwellers along the route' and attributes the delay in completion to the treacherous nature of the soil along the whole line. The heights running east to west through the island represent a singular geological structure; this feature hoists up the earlier chalk deposits to form the downland of the southern part of the island behind Ventnor, with the clays to the north forming a much more recent and less consolidated deposit. This imparts an instability for which the original contractor was ill-prepared. The *Isle of Wight Observer* was a keen if impatient supporter of the scheme, once it was under way, and was scathing in the event of delay or failure – "*We have from the first, advocated the introduction of a well arranged railway system into the Isle of Wight, believing, as we do, that railways, by the civilised spirit of the age, are now required to be established in every business locality and fashionable neighbourhood in the British Empire, and that such parts as remain without them suffer more or less from their absence.*"

Despite this averred support, the paper had in 1861 viewed 'the Approaching Railway Campaign' rather sniffily, remaining loftily above the 'trade' interests engaged in vulgar struggle. Its relish at the associated rancour and machinating was however impossible to hide.

Traffic commenced on Monday 16th June 1862 but the formal opening was to take place on the following Thursday, the 19th. The general excitement by now generated, largely made nonsense of such fine distinctions – crowds would have begun forming with the dawn that Monday. The formal opening speeches graced by a few titles and a general gathering of the Great And Good of Cowes and Newport, was reported by the *Observer* in the most extraordinary way. Ignoring the *hoi polloi* jostling for a glimpse, it chose instead to report the event only in the context of the handful of *respectable* people present. This was the 'scarce half dozen' which has been interpreted down the years as a very poor turnout –

4–4–0T, IWCR No.7, at Newport in ancient days.

No.2, PRECURSOR that was, at Newport in Isle of Wight Central Railway days.

what the report said was 'scarce half dozen' ... *worthy of consideration;* so much for the rest.

Eight trains were run that day, two of the 'persons' in the first one being W. Mollett, a local banker who was also a Director of the Cowes Floating Bridge Company, and Michael Ratsey, the yacht builder of sod cutting fame. About 600 'people' as opposed to 'persons worthy of consideration' were in fact carried that day; laurel, bunting and a few banners adorned both stations and some two thousand people took part (one way or another) in the general celebrations and rejoicing. A pair of 2-2-2 well tanks, *Pioneer* and *Precursor* (from Slaughter Gruning & Co of Bristol) worked the first services, with *Precursor,* for one, on the first day 'gaily decorated with laurels, evergreens, pennants and flags on either side'.

In August of the first year, 1862, the Board met again in *The Fountain* where it was nevertheless made known that the line was not yet complete, nor all the land transferred. Payment for construction of works to June 1862 totalled £28,955 and by July traffic was said to 'exceed every anticipation' and now that the novelty had subsided somewhat the line maintained a steady traffic of nearly 300 persons daily.

A mishap occurred at Cowes as early as March 1863 when a coach (taken by horse, note) as far as the Mill Hill tunnel 'ran back on the gradient, smashed the crossing gates at Cross Street, jumped a pile of sleepers and finished up against the station house'.

By July 1864 the service was as follows:

Cowes to Newport:
6.15   9.0   10.15 12.15   2.0   3.15   5.45   7.15   9.15

Sundays:
10.15   2.30   4.30   8.0

Newport to Cowes:
6.35   9.20   11.45 12.45   2.45   4.45   6.45   8.0   9.45

Sundays:
10.30   3.0   5.0   9.30

Fares for a single journey were: 1st Class, 1s, 2nd Class 9d. A double journey = 1st Class 1/6d, 2nd Class 1/2d. "Children over 3 years and under 12, half the above fare. Through tickets issued by Rail and Coach to and from Ventnor and Cowes".

Ex–Brighton Terriers enlivened the island fleet at one time; No.10 COWES, already redundant on the LBSCR, came over as early as 1900, to be sent back to the mainland in the middle 1930s. Newport again, works buildings beyond.

To the great majority of us now, Isle of Wight locos mean the O2 0–4–4 tanks: this is BONCHURCH at the rambling Newport coal stage in August 1952. The 'British Railways' was added, it was considered locally 'with indecent haste'. Photograph J. Davenport.

COWES

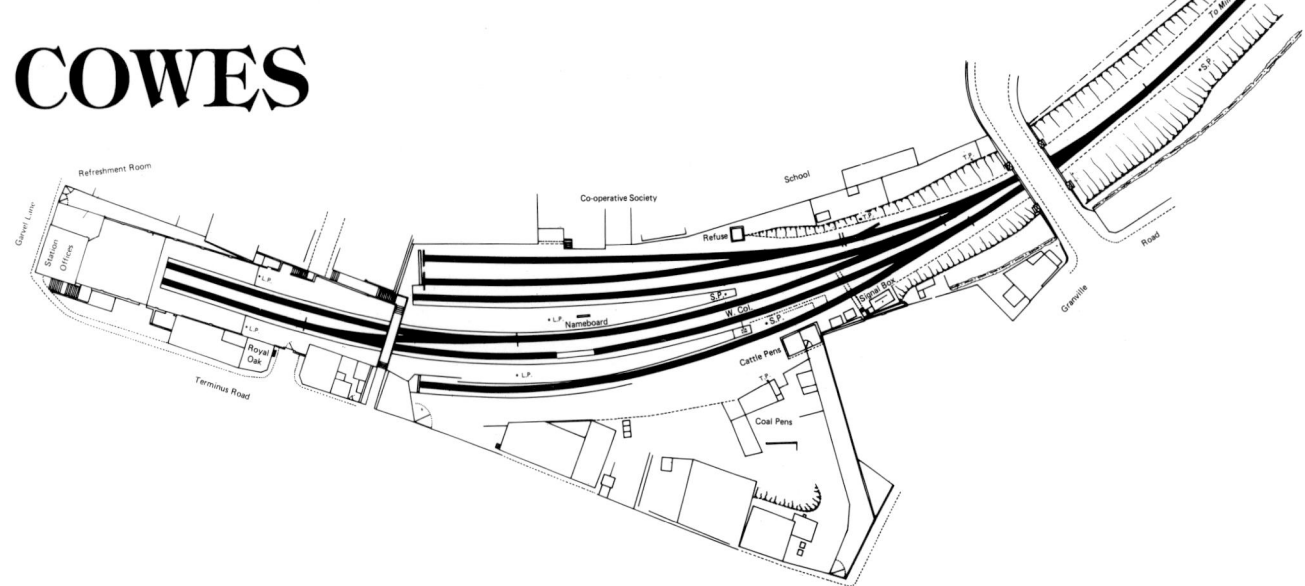

Curving round from Granville Bridge (see plan above) the railway crossed St. Mary's Road on a similar trough girder bridge. This is No.20 SHANKLIN in June 1965; in the 1880s the company had announced itself prepared to build the bridge subject to a contribution from the Ward Estate and the Town Board. There was a complementary deal involving a parcel of land ('about 28 square yards') in Cross Street by the terminus and by 17th December 1890 it was apparently finished or nearly so, for Col. Rich of the Board of Trade required the company to fix a check rail on 'the new underbridge' at Cowes. Photograph T.P. Cooper.

The Cowes station frontage; a less than imposing structure it resembled nothing so much as a very down at heel solicitor's office, whose chief partner had taken to the bottle perhaps. The picture illustrates nicely the peculiar slanting situation. Ignore the 'Southern Railway' signing – the year is 1965! 'Authority' at Waterloo, as far as the island was concerned, was a long way off, both figuratively and actually. Photograph T.P. Cooper.

22 BRADING at Cowes on the 1.28pm to Ryde, 24th June 1961. The wrought iron footbridge, for so long perhaps the most attractive feature at Cowes, seems to have its origins in the work and land purchases of 1875/76. Cross Street ran across the line on the level when the station was first built, an inconvenience awkwardly close to the platform ends. The platforms were indeed markedly short, covered, if earliest plans can be believed, by an overall wooden canopy. The company negotiated to block up Cross Street to enable extensions of the platforms and by way of a *quid pro quo* provided a pedestrian 'right of passage'. A mean terrace, unsavoury and unhealthy, lay at the top of Cross Street, the outside privies draining down the hill and away in a manner unrewarding of investigation. In 1879 the houses were being pulled down, and the pedestrian right of way replaced with a footbridge. The first bridge was accordingly put up in 1881 and was of relatively primitive construction, executed like much of the station, in wood. The rebuilding of 1891 saw it replaced in wrought iron and extended into Cross Street. The Cowes footbridge was thus never part of the station – it added much to appearances at Cowes but was nevertheless wholly separate, a crossing of the *station* rather than the running lines *per se.*

Left. Cowes as it came to be known, through to the end of steam. Fossilised throughout Southern and BR days, it dated from 1891. This is one corner, tacked on at the very top of the hill and demonstrating the curious effect of the steep slope on the relative levels. There was much local concern about expansion at the time, when the essential step was taken of enlargement to two tracks. As if the battles of Hog Lane and skirmishes with the slaughterhouse were not enough, a protracted struggle with the Cowes Board ensued, related, as usual, to money. A Public Meeting was held on 3rd February 1890 with Local Board members and 'various ratepayers' in attendance. The Cowes Board it was stated 'did not want to object for the sake of objecting' to the company's proposals, which were; 'to extend the line to the High Street and to do this they would purchase the property from the corner of Railway Street to Bishops shoe shop crossing Carvel Lane to get there.' In the event the railway never crossed Carvel Lane and there is every likelihood that this was straightforward kiteflying by the railway... Photograph T.P. Cooper.

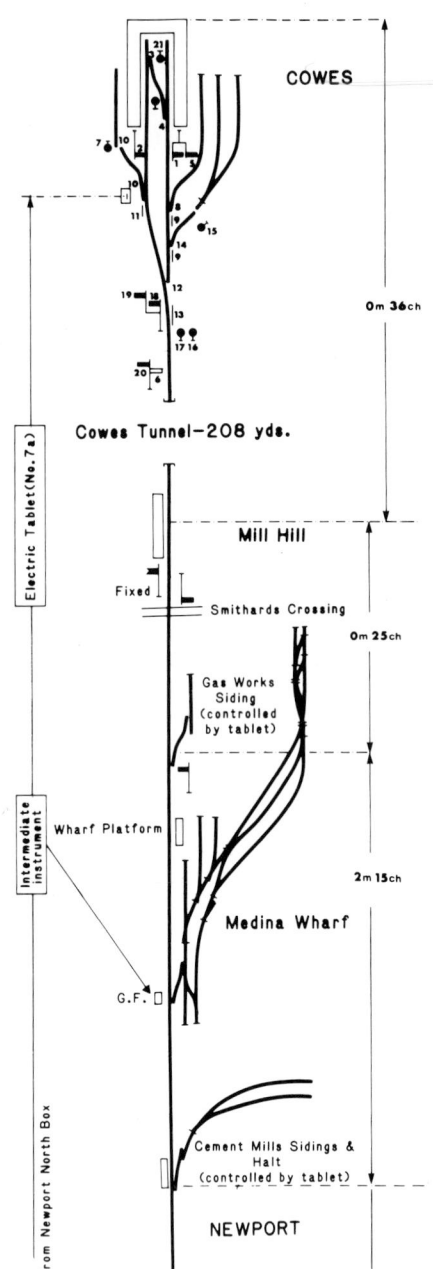

The town from the 'station' footbridge on 21st April 1957. Terraced houses continued to huddle round about the station despite the Hog Lane clearances of early years. Its yachting associations have largely obscured the doggedly industrial past of Cowes; 'Not only is Cowes the main port in the Isle of Wight, through which most of the seaborne merchandise passes, but, with the East Cowes, it forms the chief industrial centre. For centuries, ship building has been carried on there. The well–known firm of Messrs. John Samuel White and Co. which was established in 1694, is the oldest private shipyard on the Admiralty list. In recent years the aviation industry has been greatly developed at the port and the amphibian and other aircraft designed and built by Messrs Saunders-Roe and the Spartan Aircraft Co. have gained world-wide fame.' Photograph Derek Clayton.

31 CHALE flits about, to the general mystification of holidaymakers, at Cowes on 26th June 1955. Passengers arriving here – and in the mid–1950s most sunseekers still found their way to their holiday idyll *by train* – found Cowes station an unprepossessing introduction indeed. The prominent signs of coal merchants, T. Gange & Sons, and Brickwoods Ales were not the most romantic introduction to *Eden's Isle.* Photograph A.E. Bennett.

The concourse at Cowes in 1965; as with much else of the structure, it dated from the work of 1891: the battles at the time between the railway and the local Cowes worthies was touched upon earlier, on page 13. The Cowes authorities, really, wanted something out of the deal: 'It was only right the Board should receive something for the land which was the property of the town' it was declared. The Cowes and Newport appear to have proposed moving the station closer in to the town more or less as a negotiating ploy. Cost of the alterations was eventually set, in September 1890, at £2,663.14s.5d, 'exclusive of land (and property thereon) and signalling'. By April 1891 work on the new station was well under way. Nothing went well – 'The leaky condition of Cowes glass roof' was noted in June 1892 and Saxby & Farmer, having completed the signalling, were involved in a dreary, if inevitable, wrangle with the Isle of Wight Central over a disputed final amount – £6.16s. Photograph T.P. Cooper.

No.22 BRADING after arrival from Ryde Pier, 9th August 1965. Platform 2 was seldom used after 1956 except by the mail train in the last years from 1964, despite there being no direct access to the van outside. The stock was berthed here all day, except on a Sunday. Prior to 1964 a spare coach was normally parked at this point. Principal improvement of 1891, as we have seen, was the doubling of the line into the station; with work under way the *County Press* could report that year: *'The front in Carvel Lane is to be completely remodelled and a large wing added, the entrance to be at the side nearest the Catholic Chapel, thus doing away with the flight of stairs leading up to the present platform. On the left will be a large waiting room, with a staircase leading up to the platform. Over this is the reception room on a level with the platform, besides two more waiting rooms and a ladies room, the Booking Office and other offices. The line will be a double one and the wooden bridge will be replaced by one which will extend into Cross Street. The platform will be extended beyond the present coal yard and will be at least 400 feet in length and the covered part 199 feet. The front facing the Catholic Chapel and the opposite side will be entirely new and not only will the new station be a great improvement as far as the appearance is concerned, but it will be a great convenience to the travelling public."* Photograph T. Wright.

It had been the practice to run coaches in under gravity, rendering the more familiar signals, box etc. unnecessary and the first signal box proper, it seems, appeared as part of the 1891 work. On rearrangements in 1918 it was moved to its new position (above), extended at the Newport end and set on a taller brick base, to improve the signalman's outlook. Photograph A.E. Bennett.

31 CHALE makes a bit of a fuss alongside platform 1. Date around September/October 1965. Photograph T.P. Cooper.

It will have become clear from the foregoing pages that the Isle of Wight Central, and the Cowes and Newport before it, for that, paid little heed to architectural niceties and though the island railways might enjoy picturesque–ness in abundance this was a by product only, as a hard headed (well, hardish) business undertaking struggled against the odds to make a living. Reference has been made to the closing up of Cross Street – this is how it was done, an ugly blank wall bringing the road abruptly to a halt! The photographs also illustrate better the role of the footbridge – a replacement for the level crossing, definitely not a station footbridge... Photograph T.P. Cooper.

Cowes in one of its frequent periods of quietude. The Southern invested much in the island lines in the 1920s; the products of the Exmouth Junction concrete works were pouring forth and any number of items in this brave new material can be spotted in photographs taken all over the island. Little things things betray the hand of the Southern – the concrete bridge sign for instance, denoting that the Cross Street footbridge was registered at Waterloo as number 42.

FRESHWATER again, awaiting departure by platform 1, 5th December 1965. This platform sufficed for much of the off season working at Cowes and 1 constituted, if you like, 'the working station'. Any departure from platform 3 usually indicated (though practice varied over the years) an overnight berthing of the stock, held in Platform 3 road to avoid fouling light engine movements on Platform 1 and 2 roads. The 'Coal Wharf', was officially termed the 'Down Siding'. The two sidings beyond Platform 3 were officially 'Up Siding 1' and 'Up Siding 2'. Photograph A.E. Bennett.

35 FRESHWATER departing Cowes for Ryde – someone having forgotten to move the headcode discs from the opposite end! Photograph T.P. Cooper.

Shunting wagons at Cowes at 5.30 in the morning – an indication of the devotion of the photographer – around May/June 1965. The view is from the Granville Road bridge, looking towards the St Mary's Street underbridge (see earlier). The Granville Bridge caused all manner of problems over the years. It had originally been a lightly built wooden footbridge but in the late 1880s the Town had wanted to make it 'fit for vehicular traffic'. By 1894 it was noted 'in a dangerous condition'. In 1882 locks had been ordered on the gates which protected the then occupation bridge. It was desired to keep it locked when not in use 'to lessen the risk of accidents and to prevent nuisances and the other objectionable purposes to which the bridge is exposed when left unattended'. The usual squabbles and intrigue followed and the new bridge was not formally opened (by Mrs. Snellgrove, wife of the Chairman of the UDC) until 1907, at a ceremony on Wednesday 27th March, at 3.00pm. It was decorated with flags and a white ribbon was cut. Photograph T.P. Cooper.

24 (formerly CALBOURNE) rolling over the St Mary's Road, 28th August 1965. Photograph T.P. Cooper.

MILL HILL

An idea for some kind of stopping place in the vicinity of Parkhurst was briefly floated before the Cowes and Newport line opened, but for the first years the only stations proper were at the extremities of the line, the simple termini of Newport and Cowes. Despite a less than favourable financial prospect a new station at Mill Hill, near Cowes, was nevertheless soon under consideration. The Directors, forsaking the *Fountain Hotel* for the new Board Room at Cowes station, met in August 1869 and noted gloomily that the company was getting further into debt 'and could not hope to do otherwise until the line was extended beyond Newport'. A year later income was 'going from bad to worse'. On 14th May 1871 the engineer attended the Board at Cowes and reported the new station 'on the line near Mill Hill' to be 'complete and ready for opening'. The Board ordered it made ready for traffic 'forthwith', that it should be formally named Mill Hill and that fares thence to Newport would be 'the same as from Cowes'. View is trough tunnel towards Cowes, 16th February 1966. Photograph Tony Wright.

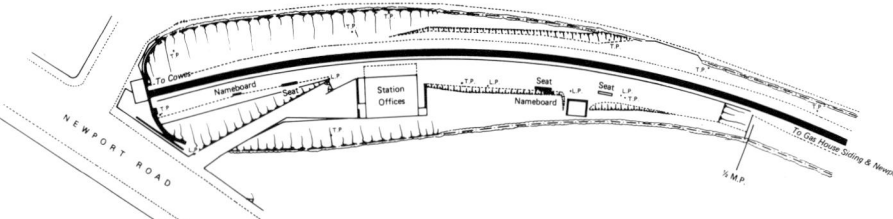

Plan, Mill Hill, 1925

Mill Hill tunnel was short and shallow, cut one suspects more in deference to the imposing Westhill House and the salubrious villas off Mill Hill Road. They had appeared from about 1848, construction taking place over some twenty years. The Westhill Estate was divided up and laid for housing from about 1890, the House itself finally being pulled down in the 1930s. Many of the 200 navvies employed on construction of the Cowes and Newport were put to work on the tunnel, the excavated earth used for embankments elsewhere on the line. View is south from tunnel, 25th December 1964. Photograph T.P Cooper.

FRESHWATER arriving at Mill Hill from Cowes in about 1964. The land above the tunnel was the subject of litigation (few developments were *not* subject to litigation on the Cowes & Newport) though the precise nature of the conflict is unclear. It possibly concerned the loss of building land – the brickwork was too shallow to permit construction over the course of the tunnel. It is far too close to the surface to have been bored conventionally, yet from the shape is not a 'cut and cover'. The guess of Tim Cooper has much logic to commend it – the clay was particularly difficult here and the tunnel was probably built on the 'sewer' principle; digging a trench, constructing a 'sewer' and filling in above. The alternative would have involved two bridges, Mill Hill Road and Newport Road and more importantly, a troublesome cutting in between. Photograph T.P. Cooper.

MERSTONE on Cowes – Ryde train at Mill Hill in the winter of 1965/1966. Photograph T.P. Cooper.

Mill Hill, looking towards Cowes on 21st April 1957. 'Mill Hill' had existed years before Cowes began its encroachment, taking over and incorporating the district. The first simple platform and building (probably in wood) burnt down within a few years, in 1879, an unfortunate occurrence recorded now only through the subsequent squabble between the railway and the Cowes Fire Brigade over the formers' refusal to pay the costs of putting out the fire! The station in this, its final form, dates from 1880/1881; the earlier building lay some yards further towards Newport and the southern–most end of the platform incorporated part of the old one. The wooden shelter was not well favoured and was disused over many years, a relic possibly of the old station, or some interim provision. When Mill Hill station was demolished, the awning was removed to reveal a stone carving, '1881' – now in the custody of the Wight Locomotive Society at Havenstreet. Photograph Derek Clayton.

Mill Hill on 21st April 1957, view is towards Newport. Photograph Derek Clayton.

Up empty stock working passing Mill Hill in January 1966. The station really served the residential outskirts of Cowes, convenient chiefly for the floating bridge linking West and East Cowes. Some dozen trains called on weekdays over many decades; a few apparently 'by signal only'. It was hardly bustling, the pace if anything languid. Apart from peak occasions of course, this was true of Cowes itself, and for years the two stations more or less shared the traffic. Parcels and luggage at Mill Hill could not compare at all with that dealt with at Cowes but the numbers of passengers was roughly the same. Photograph T.P. Cooper.

31 CHALE approaching Mill Hill station, from Newport, in June 1965. 'Arctic Road' ran alongside the line (down to Medina Wharf) and for many years a siding 109ft in length occupied the curving strip of land between the fence and the running line. It seems to have been put in before 1885 when 'Wood & Co. Coal Merchants' were recorded as conducting their business from Mill Hill station. It was removed some time after 1913 with almost the only reference to its existence contained in the report of a derailment of 26th January 1900. The 8.30am Newport – Cowes 'split the points at Mill Hill Siding (the points faced Newport) and '...passengers were forced to alight at the station. Their companions at Cowes, anticipating the 8.45 departure, had to make their own way to Mill Hill, a train being found to work back to Newport around 9.15'. Trains terminated at Mill Hill all day, the first working through to Cowes being the 6.20pm ex–Newport. Photograph T.P. Cooper.

SMITHARDS LANE

A nineteenth century institution, the Cowes Gasworks enjoyed extensions and enlargements from time to time up until 1907. It was not served by rail, having a separate loading pier on the Medina. 'A level Crossing' was made on the railway nearby in 1880, assumed to be 'Smithards Crossing', after a smithy which had existed since before 1820. This is it, in 1965. Photograph T.P. Cooper.

Plan, Smithards Lane, 1925

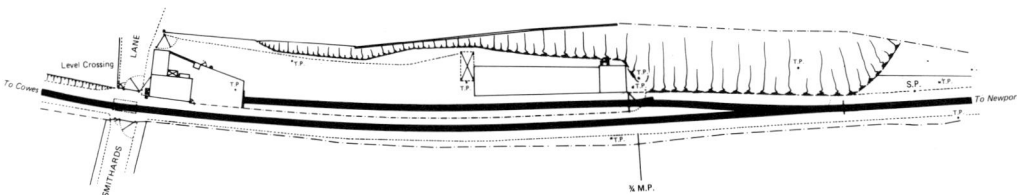

Smithards Lane crossing, No.29 ALVERSTONE passing, in 1964; the gasworks lay to the left and the land slopes away eastwards down to the river. Beyond the Lane to the left (i.e. the east) of the line a siding was eventually built. 'A Residential Crossing Keeper' was at Smithards through to BR days and as early as 1889 the Board of Trade's Colonel Hutchinson had expressed himself unhappy about the arrangements; he suggested a footbridge and the company compromised by resolving to fix a warning notice and bell on the keeper's house. The place was slightly odd, in that it was an occupation rather than a public level crossing; consequently the gates were normally kept closed, a local bone of some contention over the years. Photograph T.P. Cooper.

Smithards Lane Crossing in 1964. The uphill gate opened across the line, that 'down' the hill necessarily outwards, away from the railway. Footgates were provided at one side for pedestrians, the keeper emerging on the ring of the automatic bell, to pull the lever locking the gates – the crossing opened to vehicles only 'on request' and locals usually found it more expedient to drive round past Mill Hill station. Smithards Crossing was protected by stop signals only, no distants, both of which operated off the same lever. Photograph T. M. Cooper.

Beyond Smithards Lane (see plan opposite) lay 'Gas Housing Siding' – at 201ft. 6in. it held eleven trucks and was protected by a scotch block, the points facing Newport. Its title was something of a misnomer in that it served as a conventional domestic distribution siding only, named for its close proximity to the gas works, rather than any particular association with it. It seems originally to have dealt with coke, for disposal throughout the island. Earliest references are dated 23rd September 1890 when it was reported that 'the site for the new siding at Gasworks, Cowes, had been inspected by the Chairman and Mr. Martin and that instructions have been given for construction to proceed.' By 1920 it served a coal merchant, a Mr. W.T. Mahy being in occupation. This seems to have been in succession to the Mill Hill siding and seems finally to have gone out of use around the end of 1964, or early in 1965. One of the Isle of Wight Railway Beyer Peacock 2-4-0Ts was broken up there in the 1920s. View dated 25th December 1965 – a further instance of the intrepidity of our photographer. Photograph T.P. Cooper.

MEDINA WHARF
'The Jetty'

There was constant animosity, from before the days of the railway, between Cowes and Newport; their relative prosperity depended upon the Medina and the degree to which each town served as a landing point. The situation was further soured and complicated by certain rights exercised by Newport over the harbour at Cowes, to the fury of the latter. The railway suffered through this rivalry, and was eyed with suspicion by some Newport interests, regarding it as a device to loosen the Newport hold.

For its earliest ingress to the island the Cowes and Newport Railway had made use of Medham Hard, which lies about 1½ miles up river from Cowes. Construction of the line had begun southwards from Cowes and on reaching the Hard it was possible to unload *Precursor* and *Pioneer*. This was merely making use of an existing, largely unsatisfactory, landing place and powers to construct a proper wharf in the immediate district were sought in 1869. The Bill, for 'a jetty at Shamblers', had to be withdrawn when Newport Corporation demanded compensation of £1,000, forcing the company the following year to make use of Medham Hard again, for the importation of its new locomotive, an 0-4-2 saddle tank, *Mill Hill*. The operation ended in disaster when *Mill Hill* toppled into the Medina mud and stuck fast. *Isle of Wight Observer, 12th March 1870*:

Plan, Medina Wharf, 1924

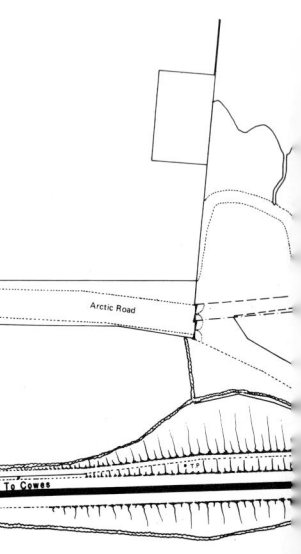

And quiet flows the Medina. Island self-reliance over the years has made for a wagon fleet where 'make do and mend' shows to an unusual extent — there is scarcely an unrepaired wagon in sight. View is northwards, summer of 1964. Photograph T.P. Cooper.

Reconstruction, Southern Railway

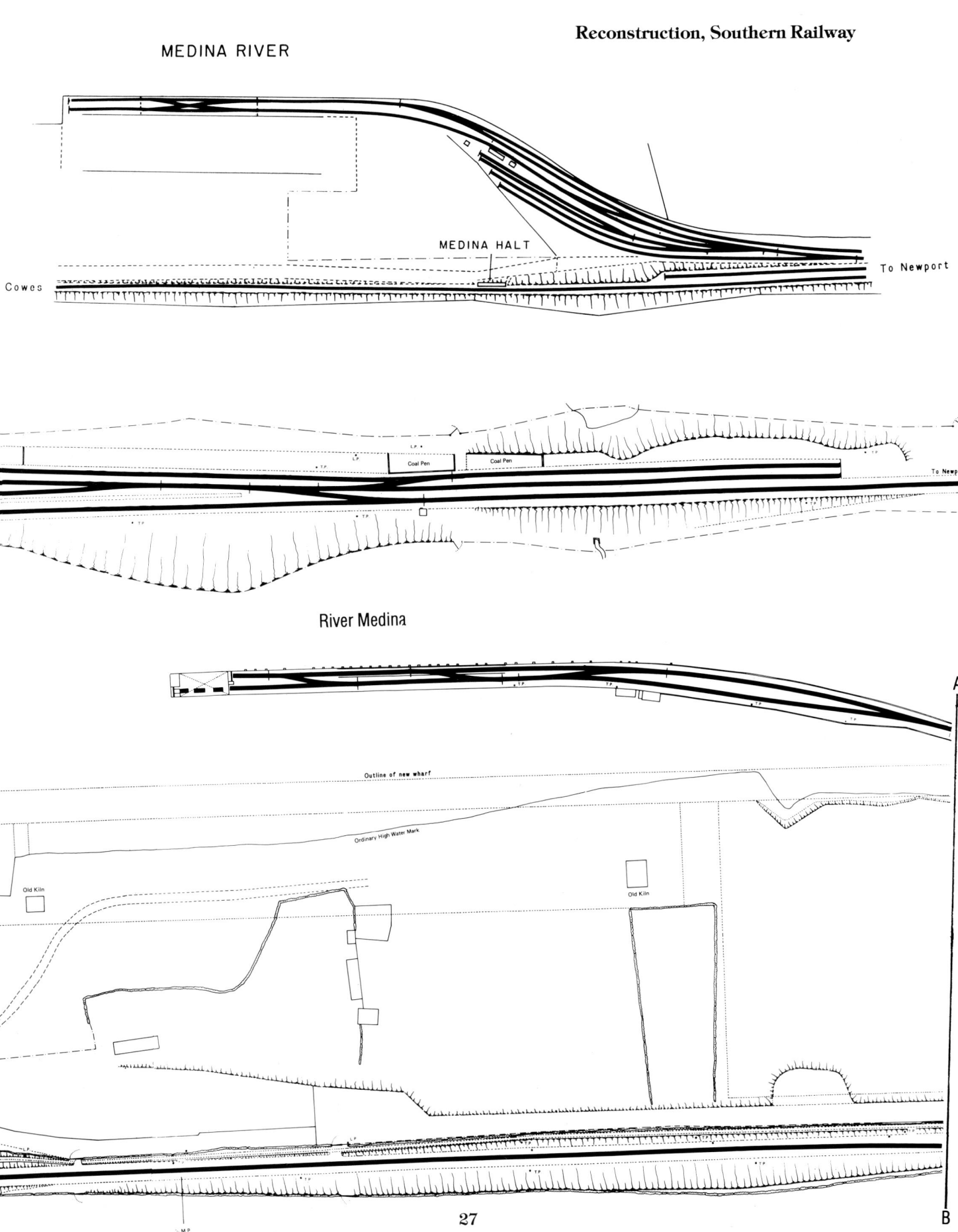

Accident to a Locomotive

On Friday 4th March as several men in the employ of the Cowes and Newport Railway were endeavouring to get a new locomotive on shore, which had just been received from the makers at Birmingham,* the gear which they had trusted to get it on shore proved too weak to sustain its weight and the engine was precipitated into the mud on the river side where the tide when it was high could flow completely round it. Efforts were, of course, made to get it out, but without avail and on Saturday and Sunday passengers by rail could see the engine on its side with the water up all around it.

Mill Hill was finally retrieved and later became the regular shunting locomotive (as 'No. 3') on the new Medina Wharf.

A Bill for the Parliamentary Session of 1875 concerning works on the Cowes and Newport and the Ryde and Newport Railways contained references again to a 'Wharf near Shamblers'. There is little detail available concerning the construction of the Wharf, with references absent, in the curious manner which seems to have attended most major events in the development of the line. The work was prolonged through the unhelpfulness of the Borough of Newport, with a lengthy row over compensation for loss of trade. The Company was forced to put in a low level siding at Newport so that wagons could get onto the quay there; unnecessary and almost never used the company subsequently had to endure demands from the Town for its removal. Medina Wharf seems to have finally opened in November 1878, locally always known as 'Medina Jetty' or simply

At the jetty was a wooden halt; it enjoyed a sort of twilight existence, intended for staff only but probably useful at times for others in the know. There were two shifts at Medina (latterly at least) and the halt could remain open well into the night, the gloom pierced only by a single inadequate electric lamp. It does not appear on Ordnance Surveys of 1896 and 1907 but reference does exist in the *Isle of Wight Herald* for 21st January 1910, to 'the Jetty Station'. It formally closed with the rest of the line on 20th February 1966. Photograph T.P. Cooper.

The layout at Medina Wharf changed considerably in its detail over the years but essentially comprised a headshunt and run round arrangements, exiting on to the main line for Newport. This is No.1 MEDINA, an appropriately–named E1 0–6–0T wholly unlike the 02s which inhabit most of the rest of these pages, shunting the wharf on 7th July 1955. The sidings here were lower than the main line and dropped down further to the quay itself. The transporters are visible beyond the trees. The long siding, more or less level with the main line, was used to marshall heavy trains, avoiding the 'hoist' up the steep grade out of the wharf. After World War II the Southern brought over 88 13 ton 8–plank open wagons to replace old LBSCR examples condemned through wartime arrears of maintenance. They had steel underframes and were higher than the LBSC wagons, a markedly evident disparity. Photograph P.J. Kelley.

'The Jetty'.

Completion of an early 'extension' was described as 'expected' by a delegate to the Committee of Management on 1st May 1880. The jetty was executed mainly in wood; the company had hardly been in a position to lavish a fortune on its construction and by the 1890s its condition was giving rise to some considerable concern. In March 1896, in evidence on the state of Cowes Harbour, a Mr. Shelford, M.I.C.E. declared that "Shamblers Jetty is in a very unsafe condition ... it is constructed of piles braced together. Some of the piles have been eaten through and will not carry the weight of an ordinary locomotive, although a smaller one is on it" [the luckless *Mill Hill*, by now No.3]. "Two steamers" he went on "could not get alongside and there are no appliances for unloading more than one". The company (now the Isle of Wight Central) had at least requested the Board of Trade to hold an inquiry into the condition of the Wharf, which despite problems of safety and convenience was proving a worthwhile investment – a road to it was 'now being constructed'. Repairs, apparently only of a desultory kind, were put in hand during the summer of 1896.

An unpleasant winter followed and 'a portion' of the jetty collapsed on 20th January 1897. 'Its condition has been a matter of concern for some time' it was glumly noted. Some repair work must have been carried out though again it could not have amounted to much. The 'Central' could never afford the necessary rebuilding and at the Board meeting of October 1903 further doubts were expressed about the precarious nature of the structures. £100 was approved on 27th September 1911 for 'additional piles' which presumably stayed the worst and in June the following year further alterations were ordered to ease the working of the wharf. Extra sidings were ordered with land from the Ward Estate bought at "a nominal charge subject to construction of a 20ft. roadway (£75) eventually to be connected by the Estate to one of the public roads in Cowes." This roadway amounted to a gravel single track, from the Jetty, which was originally accessible by water only, to the end of Arctic Road. Other conditions included access across the line to the oyster beds. 'The works may cost us £525', a gloomy Board heard.

'The Jetty' by 1923, at the end of the Central's existence, was a rambling structure, less than adequate for its chief commodity – coal, and awkward and untrustworthy for the landing of major items like engines. Broke, the Isle of Wight Central could not contemplate the large scale renewal necessary and no help would be forthcoming from local interests. The transformation of Medina Wharf had to await the advent of the Southern Railway in 1923, when a new concrete jetty formed only one part of a considerable investment programme, designed to put the entire island system into (relatively) good shape.

*A reporting error; the engine came from Black, Hawthorn of Gateshead.

24, formerly CALBOURNE, at Medina Junction in January 1966. The wharf attracts various entries in the archives over the years – 'Additional accommodation' in 1901 drew the ever-unwelcome attention of Newport Council, with threats to invoke awkward clauses 'in the Ryde and Newport Act 1877'. 'Wharfinger White' retired in July 1901 and Conacher in contradiction of the latter day definition at least (Wharfinger – Wharf Owner) promoted Shunter Matthews in his place. In November Conacher suffered further frustration having the chance of a second hand crane 'from Pollock and Brown' (Pollock, Brown & Co. Scrap Merchants, Southampton) in exchange for 'old scrap'. The Board wanted their money first, to sell the old scrap before considering the purchase of the second hand crane... Conacher, with his flair (for publicity at least, if not for practicalities) deserved better things; the board would not even 'incur the expense' when he asked for his 'Railway Magazine' publicity pieces to be reproduced as leaflets. He left for the Cambrian, where he never achieved success, in March 1910. Photograph T.P. Cooper.

Right. Newport goods train departing Medina Junction, 1964. The Medina, swollen to a breadth unwarranted by its modest length, made its unhurried way through the flat claylands and fields which characterised of the northern half of the island – wholly unlike the breezy downs to the south. Its course was paralleled in more than one sense, by the Cowes and Newport. Photograph T.P. Cooper.

SEAVIEW at Medina Wharf, August 1965. The mudlands of the Medina were historically good oyster grounds, relatively undamaged even by the long established brick and cement industries. The Newport authorities had opposed construction of the jetty for reasons of self interest, fearing a loss of trade. Tactics at one time involved putting up the oyster people to oppose the wharf and they duly claimed on the hapless railway, who paid up. The oystermen blithely carried on their business regardless. Photograph T.P. Cooper.

'The Jetty'. Like its predecessor the new wharf (it was completed in the early 1930s) took the traditional name. The old wooden jetty had suffered much through inadequate construction, falling prey to worm and rot over the years and was demolished by February 1932. Photograph T.P. Cooper.

Medina in 1965. Principal features and attributes of the new wharf were the giant transporters – coal of course, until the 1960s, was the main fuel (especially domestically) of the island and the railway's principal freight income. Photograph T.P. Cooper.

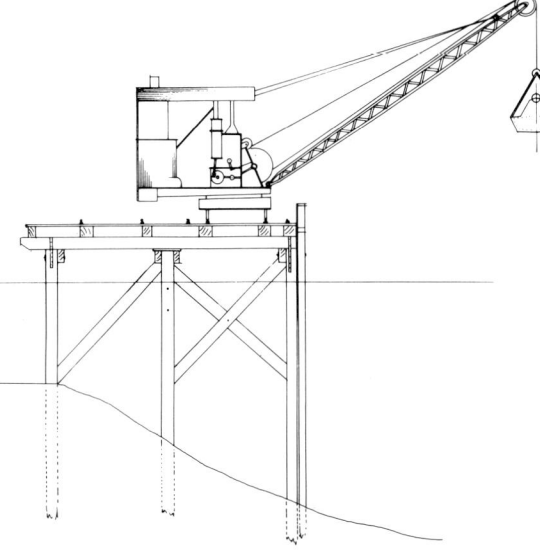

Crane drawing for old Medina Wharf – other detail unknown.

Coal on the wharf sidings in 1930. As Conacher maintained, Medina was the principal point of entry for this sort of essential traffic and the sidings were added to and extended over the years. Earliest mention of a crane is a rail mounted hand machine new from Armstrong Whitworth in January 1879. The 'Central' could in truth never hope to raise the capital necessary for any comprehensive updating of the jetty and relied upon *ad hoc* tinkerings. In August 1901 for instance a proposed new siding (one only) was ordered 'to be on the land not the water side'– which was probably just as well. Repairs had been done in 1896 and in August 1899 Conacher reported 'progress made' and requested 'authorisation for further work'. He faced daily the grim reality of hand to mouth economics. How it must have irked him, the humiliating fobbing–off of merchants' claims as to accuracy of the Medina Wharf weighbridge.

Above. SEAVIEW at Medina Wharf, October 1965.

Left. Cuckoo in the nest. Wagons for the Ryde – Shanklin electric line landing at Medina Wharf in August 1966. All the railway's own requirements too, of course, had to come by sea and this is true to the present day. The picture recalls many such incidents – the unloading of No.4 WROXALL at the new wharf on 23rd June 1933 for instance, which required (like most heavy work) the assistance of the floating crane out of Southampton. Photograph T.P. Cooper.

CALBOURNE that was, waiting to join the main line with the afternoon goods from Medina Wharf to Newport, 9th August 1965. Photograph Tony Wright.

The collier CAMBERWAY alongside the old jetty, illustrating the primitive and time consuming method of transferring coal (and other stuff). Nevertheless this had served the island well as Charles Conacher explained in his *opus, Multum in Parvo* 1899: "Aided by three powerful steam cranes and all other necessary appliances, the Co. were able to effect the discharge of 122 steam colliers in 1898, representing a tonnage into trucks of 73,000 tons. With the most complete facilities, we can deal with boats of 1,000 tons burden with ease and despatch, and colliers of large tonnage trade regularly throughout the year between the wharf and the Welsh and Tyne ports."

CEMENT MILLS

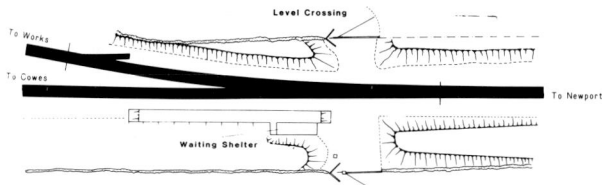

Plan, Cement Mills Halt, 1942

Plan, opposite page. Brickyards and kilns were an ancient feature of the west bank of the Medina, a strip of intermittent industrial activity which included an early cement mill. Charles Francis and Sons had evidently been established since the early 1800s, the new line passing on a viaduct close the their 'West Medina Mill'. So it was labelled on the 1863 survey and the Southampton Times had reported it being 'enlarged substantially' in April 1862.

Cement on the Medina was a major endeavour, Francis' products finding a wide market and not just in Britain. The firm made application (refused) to the Cowes and Newport Railway as early as the 1860s to lay 'a tram road' across the main line to their clay grounds inland from the river. The tramway was subsequently built, being taken under the railway in 1871. The works continued an expansion as the island railways came together and permission was obtained for a new underline bridge for the tramway in March 1895. An iron bridge still exists (at least it did until recently) bearing an 1895 Westwood and Winley plate; the 1871 bridge it replaced was presumably built in wood. The Francis company owned the Pan pit at Shide, whence trains of wagons loaded with chalk would be propelled through Newport station to the works. Operations within the works had become enormously complex with a number of narrow gauge systems but production, it would appear, peaked long before the outbreak of the Second World War. The works closed in 1944 but the quay remained in use, the Blue Circle company maintaining some facilities there, although the site was largely derelict. The halt (unlike Medina Wharf) was a public one, though it was never advertised and was used by fishermen and the occupants of the nearby isolated cottages. A sailing school set up at nearby Dodnor around 1960 also generated some traffic.

Above. Offices, siding and halt at Cement Mills, taken from the rear of the train in the summer of 1964. There were two halts on the line, at Medina Wharf and Cement Mills. both were intended for workers at the two main Medina commercial undertakings and both are of decidedly uncertain origin. A platform at least seems to have existed for the Francis Co. Mills prior to the 1890s. In April of 1891 a man was killed in a fall from the nearby viaduct; in the inquest it was revealed that coming from Cowes *he had taken a ticket only as far as Cement Mills* but alighted at Newport and paid the excess fare. In February 1879 the *Isle of Wight Chronicle* noted that trains 'conveyed passengers to Cement Mills' but the precise meaning is not clear. On 18th November 1896 the Central Board deferred the question of a 'Cement Mills Station' ... 'originally proposed in 1892' (a reference to a request from Messrs. Francis in November of that year) though demands recurred; in April 1898 the Directors read a letter from the Manager, Mr. Conacher, regarding the 'proposed new station at Cement Mills ... and this was referred to the Chairman'. The first positive reference to the halt turns up in the newspapers of 1905. Photograph T.P. Cooper.

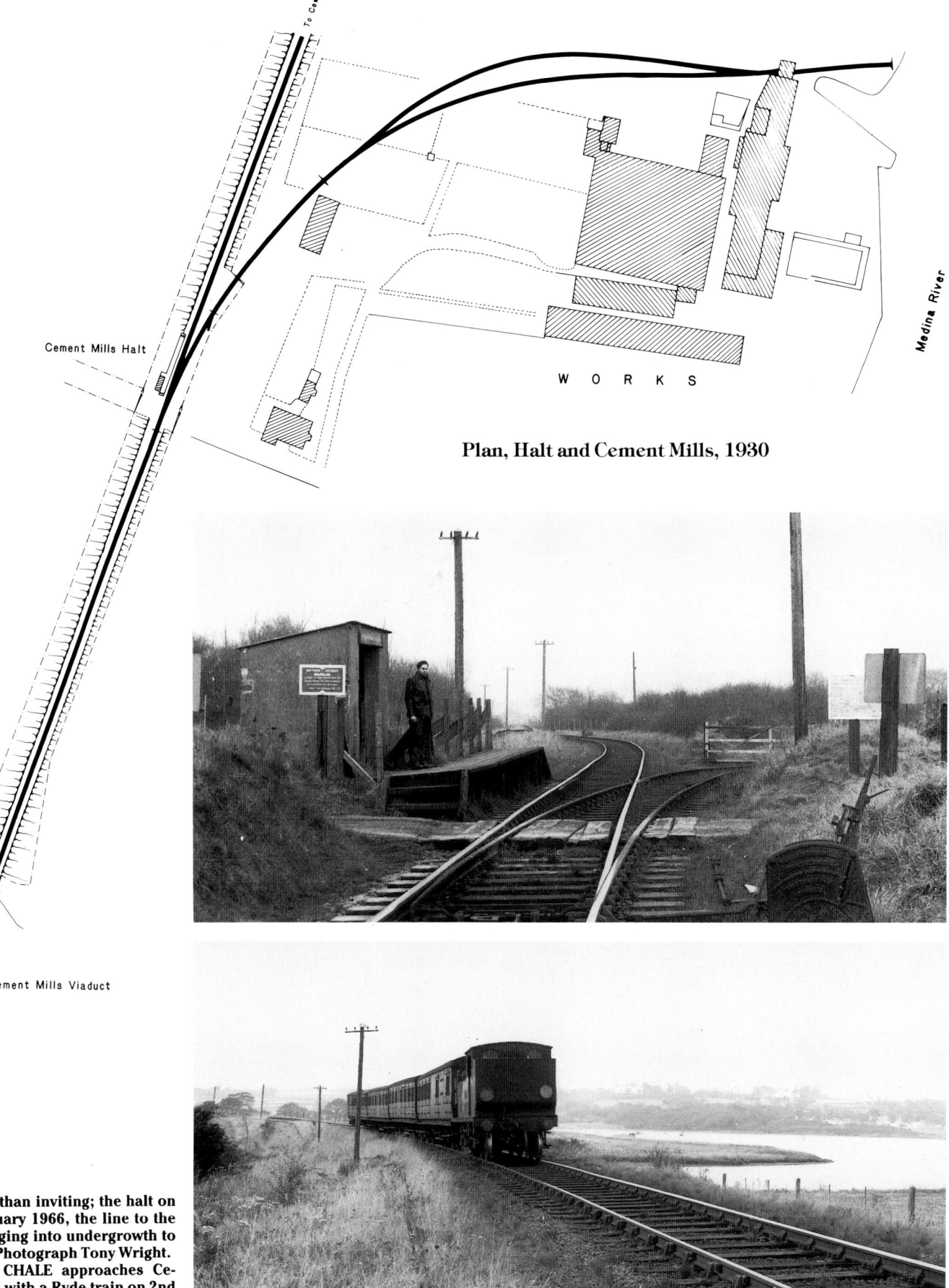

Plan, Halt and Cement Mills, 1930

Top. Less than inviting; the halt on 16th February 1966, the line to the Mills plunging into undergrowth to the right. Photograph Tony Wright.
Right. 31 CHALE approaches Cement Mills with a Ryde train on 2nd October 1965. Photograph A.E. Bennett.

No.33 BEMBRIDGE with a Medina Wharf to Newport goods (with customary much–patched wagons) crossing Cement Mills viaduct in 1964/1965. Low culverted embankments served in most circumstances but near Cement Mills the line crossed a small inlet, originally the works 'mill pond'. The viaduct at first (it would seem) was timber built, probably to the same low standard to be employed at Medina and the Bill for the Parliamentary Session 1875 included amongst its many works a proposal 'to replace the wooden viaduct … with a solid embankment properly culverted'. What eventually emerged was this iron viaduct, the most notable engineering feature on the line (view is south to Newport). Photograph T.P. Cooper.

Up train crossing Cement Mills Viaduct, 19th February 1966. The Southern Railway altered the number of the viaduct from 7 to 31 (renumbering the bridges from the opposite end of the line) and installed extra piling, the additional uprights standing clear of the viaduct and braced to the original piers. These were 'Hughes Piles', four, each 40 feet long and secondhand, having been recovered 'from Rockley Viaduct'. Photograph A.E. Bennett.

Cowes train crossing Cement Mills viaduct, 19th February 1966. The SR work was completed in June 1926 but the structure was never wholly satisfactory and a speed limit existed. 'Sway bracing', a complex girder arrangement, was considered in the 1930s and if carried out would have altered the appearance substantially. The viaduct was a convenient means of access to the Medina for fishermen who hailed a train at the halt 'by a red light' or more conventionally a simple wave. Photograph A.E. Bennett.

Up train, 1965, appearing to emerge from the reeds. After 1944, with closure of the mills, the 'pond' was steadily diminished by encroaching vegetation and sediment. Whether this was a direct consequence of the closure or not is hard to say. Photograph T.P. Cooper.

NEWPORT
and the Advent of the Central

The Cowes and Newport directors then, had perceived where long term security lay; their isolated 4½ miles of line required to be part of a proper island route, after all it amounted to only a portion of several far more extensive schemes. Early efforts had been directed at a line on to Ventnor but salvation, such as it was, came with the link across the island to Ryde, already a major point of entry from the mainland and a growing centre of trade and commerce in its own right. To this end the 'Ryde and Newport Direct Railway' had been promoted in the early 1860s, its Bill rejected by Parliament as not sufficiently grounded amongst local interests.

Proposals afterwards suffered indifferent progress under various collaborative guises until an Act was obtained in 1872 for the 'Ryde and Newport Railway'. By autumn of the following year work was 'being very rapidly pushed ahead'. For it to operate in unison with the Cowes and Newport, not only would some considerable enlargement be necessary at Newport, where the station, intended as a temporary measure, boasted only the simplest arrangements, but it would be expedient to remove the primitive workshops, stores and offices from the now-remote situation at Cowes to the more central position at Newport. In addition (as noted in the introductory text) a third line had been projected to Newport – a threadbare concern entitled the Isle of Wight (Newport Junction) Railway, inching its course to insolvency from Sandown in fits and starts during the 1870s.

The Cowes and Newport secretary announced to the Board on 2nd May 1872 that Bills for both the Ryde and Newport and Isle of Wight and Newport Junction Railways had passed the Lords, and also had news of yet a fourth concern, a line across the claylands to the west, to Freshwater and Yarmouth. This too would require accommodation at Newport. A month after 'provisional agreement' had been reached with the Ryde and Newport and throughout the year the Board busied itself with a variety of soundings and approaches. On occasion it met in the *Dolphin Hotel* at Cowes, finally resolving terms with the Ryde and Newport in November 1872. In December an inquiry was made of the Isle of Wight railway away on the east coast, as to the terms upon which it would work 'the Cowes and Newport and Ryde and Newport Joint Line'. At the same time the Isle of Wight (Newport Junction) Co. had enquired regarding use of the 'Joint Newport Station'. It was clear to all that a new station required to be built though of course there was little agreement on the precise siting, division of costs, or on any detail.

In February of 1873 the IWR let it be known that they were prepared to work both the Cowes and Newport and the Ryde and Newport 'for a fixed percentage'. The minutes do not record the reaction to this offer though already the Cowes and Newport Board must have examined the possibilities of working the lines itself, taking over from the engineer, Martin; indeed by the summer of 1876 arrangements were being made for the hire of his rolling stock. Martin, Civil Engineer and

Cowes train passing Shamblers Copse, Cowes, in April 1965. Photograph T.P. Cooper.

No.27 MERSTONE on a Cowes – Sandown train running into Newport on 14th September 1937. Beyond lies the Medina, seldom far from the Cowes – Newport line. Photograph S.W. Baker.

Director for much of his life, was paid in shares and ended up owning most of the Isle of Wight Central. The locomotives were among the assets in his will!

The Board of Trade were asked to assist in the settlement over the new Newport station and at the end of 1873 the C&N Board heard that Mr. Swarbrick of the Great Eastern had been appointed 'umpire ... in the matter of the site for the proposed joint station at Newport, and other purposes'. Swarbrick pondered the problem and by December came up with the unremarkable solution of distributing costs and profits equally between the three companies. An obvious course, he also determined that the new station should lay alongside the Cowes and Newport terminus, and that 'no other station' should be allowed in the town.

The minutes repeatedly fall silent at critical junctures and it is not clear exactly when the new joint station opened – quite a grand affair in comparison to its crude predecessor. December 1875 seems a reasonable date, when the Ryde and Newport opened for traffic, for the two systems must needs have come to some conjoint arrangement. Certainly the new station was working by 1878, for the Isle of Wight and Newport Junction was being pushed for its share of the costs, despite its failure so far to physically win access across the Medina.

The first Cowes and Newport Railway Board meeting held at Newport station took place on 31st August 1878. Thereafter the Board customarily convened here. A Joint Committee was the most sensible mode of disposing these close working arrangements. Its formation was originally authorised under an Act of 1872 and it seems to have been properly in operation by 1877. The Isle of Wight and Newport Junction's line spent the latter part of the 1870s in relative impotence, unable through lack of funds to extend from a temporary terminus outside Newport (at Pan Lane) to the joint station; this it finally accomplished in 1879 only to plunge into bankruptcy the following year. Its affairs were from thereon effectively the responsibility of the Joint Committee, representing now three ostensibly independent companies. Such diversity may be charming in retrospect but in reality was more than slightly absurd. 'The multifarious nature of the island's railways' was increased further by the involvement of two mainland companies, the London and South Western and the London Brighton and South Coast. Together with the Isle of Wight Railway this constituted over-complication on a scale approaching the heroic and schemes of amalgamation filled these years. One William Abbott, a London (and therefore untrustworthy) stocks and shares broker, was even put up to a 'Market Report'... *"It will be news to my readers that there are 37¼ miles of railway in the Island divided into six companies, presided over by 19 directors, 6 secretaries, legally governed by 3 solicitors, scientifically guarded by 4 engineers and skillfully administered by 4 managers. To guard (or more strictly speaking to obstruct) the interests of the 37¼ miles of railway – nearly one guardian per mile. Was there ever anything more absurd in the history of rail-*

Below. Headquarters of the Isle of Wight Central, and Conacher's realm. The station was approached past the goods yard, site of the old terminus. It was a curving lane taken off Sea Street by a part of Newport labelled 'Little London'. A bridge was necessary over the now–enfeebled Medina – the Lukely Brook long worked into a series of mill ponds. At first an inconsequential structure, probably wooden, the bridge was rebuilt between the Saturday night of 17th March 1894 and the following Monday morning, 19th March.

There can be no doubt but that Newport was a busy place – gathered together the concentration of stock could be most impressive. Its condition often left much to be desired however and the Central had essentially spread itself too widely, in the least promising parts of the island, to profit much from the traffic. With extensive new works in progress a deputation from Waterloo visited the island in 1930, when the condition of the station approach (see top photo) had if anything deteriorated: 'It was noticed that the approach to the station has a very unsightly appearance and that nothing has yet been done to make use of the frontage space between the entrance gates of the Approach Road and the station premises.' The SR Traffic Committee had authorised extensive now work in October 1926, when all the signs and the painting scheme, it was ordered, should be made to conform with standard Southern practice – green and white enamel plates and so on. The whole of the staff lobbies behind the refreshment room were ordered to be swept away and 'replaced by one corrugated iron building, constructed of second hand material'. This grand new structure would accommodate a coal store, lamps, electric and telegraph staff and a pw store.

Plan, Newport, 1925

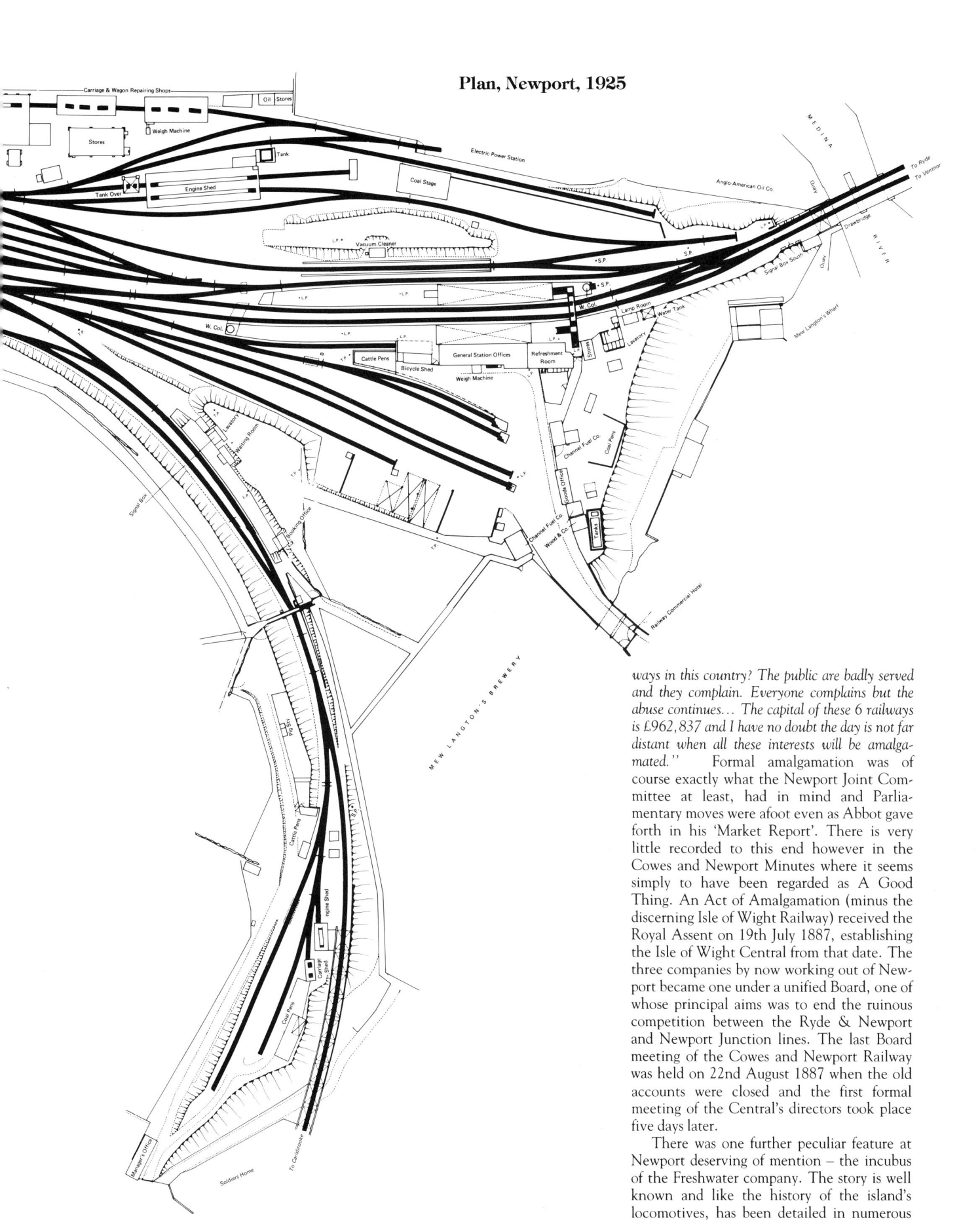

ways in this country? The public are badly served and they complain. Everyone complains but the abuse continues... The capital of these 6 railways is £962,837 and I have no doubt the day is not far distant when all these interests will be amalgamated." Formal amalgamation was of course exactly what the Newport Joint Committee at least, had in mind and Parliamentary moves were afoot even as Abbot gave forth in his 'Market Report'. There is very little recorded to this end however in the Cowes and Newport Minutes where it seems simply to have been regarded as A Good Thing. An Act of Amalgamation (minus the discerning Isle of Wight Railway) received the Royal Assent on 19th July 1887, establishing the Isle of Wight Central from that date. The three companies by now working out of Newport became one under a unified Board, one of whose principal aims was to end the ruinous competition between the Ryde & Newport and Newport Junction lines. The last Board meeting of the Cowes and Newport Railway was held on 22nd August 1887 when the old accounts were closed and the first formal meeting of the Central's directors took place five days later.

There was one further peculiar feature at Newport deserving of mention – the incubus of the Freshwater company. The story is well known and like the history of the island's locomotives, has been detailed in numerous

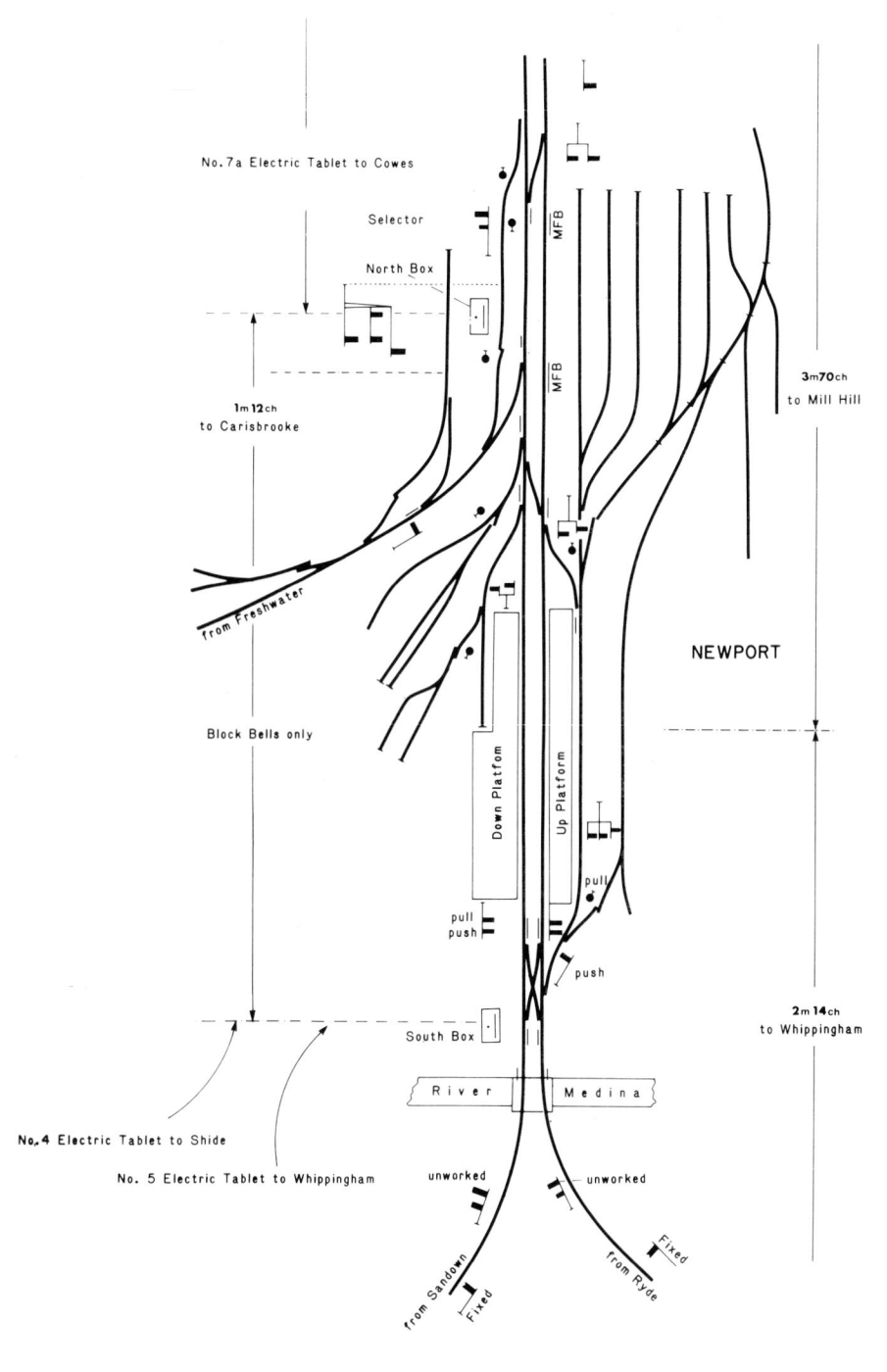

[Diagram of Newport station track layout with labels: No.7a Electric Tablet to Cowes; Selector; North Box; 1m 12ch to Carisbrooke; 3m 70ch to Mill Hill; MFB; from Freshwater; NEWPORT; Block Bells only; Down Platform; Up Platform; pull push; push; South Box; 2m 14ch to Whippingham; No. 4 Electric Tablet to Shide; No. 5 Electric Tablet to Whippingham; River Medina; unworked; unworked; Fixed; from Sandown; from Ryde; Fixed]

texts. The Freshwater, Yarmouth and Newport Railway had come to a working agreement with the Central in 1889 but relations were never exactly cordial. The little company 'broke free', setting up, ludicrously, its own ramshackle station a 100 yards or so down its own line in 1913. A solution was eventually patched up and the Great Row, avoiding the repetition of a much related tale, is probably best crystallised in these two letters; addressed to the Board of Trade they lay out, as usefully as we are likely to see anywhere, the views of the two opposing camps. The Central put the boot in first with the Board of Trade:

4th September 1913

Sir,

It will be within your knowledge that the Freshwater, Yarmouth & Newport Railway has until the 30th June last been worked by this Company from the time of its being opened in 1889. During that period in accordance with the compulsory powers obtained by the Freshwater Company by their Act of 1880 the whole of their traffic was accommodated in this Company's Station at Newport on the terms of a payment regulated by that Act. The Freshwater Company declined to renew the Working Agreement with this Company when it expired last June, and since that date under the direction of Sir Sam Fay, who has been appointed a Receiver and Manager, have worked the Line themselves.

For this purpose and with a view of refraining from the exercise of the powers of user of this Company's Station obtained by them in their Act of 1880 the Freshwater Co. have constructed a separate Station at Newport without any proper means of access by road, and before you pass the Station for public traffic it is desirable that a cart road should be provided.

(There are) only two means of access to the platform of the new Station. The first is over a switchback public footpath of an average width of 6 feet 6 inches, the entrance to which is through a gateway where the footpath joins the private approach road to this Company's Station. The distance to be travelled is 564 feet.

The second means of access is round by public roads, i.e. Holyrood Street, Crocker Street and St James Street to the Offices of the Freshwater Company at Hunnyhill, thence by the side of their Sidings along a newly formed cartpath which terminates at a gate (which is kept closed) but which opens on to one side of a footbridge over their railway. This footbridge connects the public footpath before referred to with the public footpath on the other side of the line: the distance by this route including the public road, is 2,280 feet.

On account of the situation in which the Freshwater Company have built their new Station this Company has used the first footpath for the conveyance of parcels, luggage, etc, from this Company's Station to the new Station of the Freshwater Company. Barrows have to be used for this purpose, and the Police have already summoned one of our Porters for causing an obstruction in this way on the footpath, and will probably issue further summonses if we continue to use it. If the second route was adopted our men would still be liable to be summoned for obstruction when going over the footbridge and the public footpath each side.

Passengers accompanied by their luggage have to engage the services of outside Porters for the transference of their luggage, and these outside Porters are similarly liable to be summoned for obstruction.

In the case of Invalid Passengers who cannot walk between the two Stations, they cannot be wheeled in a bath chair along the footpath without being similarly liable, and it is impossible for them to be driven from one station to the other without utilising the footpath.

I am, etc

Russell Willmott.

For Sir Sam Fay, of the Great Central, no less, this was doubtless small town stuff, and was dealt with in suitably magisterial fashion:

10th September 1913.

Sir,

As the attention of the Board of Trade has been drawn to the working of the Freshwater Company's line by that Company,

Newport staff around 1910 (the engine is No.2). By 1914 the Isle of Wight Central was running its own catering at Newport but in earlier years a contractor had been responsible. Licensing laws before the Great War were radically different from today, though inevitably some form of regulation was in force. One Charles Martin Piper 'Keeper of the Refreshment Room' fell foul of these in 1877. *Bona fide* 'travellers' could drink whilst on their way 'and by the Act any person arriving by train or intending to depart by train were entitled to be served'. Fanny Lane, the barmaid, gave evidence that on Sunday 14th October 'three young gentlemen' had come in just before three in the afternoon. She asked if they were travellers. They said they were and they had refreshment. They missed the train 'but went by the next'. Fanny's evidence was crucial, for the case was dismissed – it had come about through the investigative zeal of PC Cousins, who had surprised the three young blades... 'drinking ale and stout'... 'at 3.45 pm'. Conclusively, he had heard 'money rattling'. Fanny and her boss had got off though such moral turpitude had been predicted by local worthies long before. In 1852 a discussion class in Newport debated *The Moral Evils of Railways* which, they concluded, 'would outweigh any advantages' because of, no less: *"1. An increase of Sabbath desecration; 2. Unwholesome speculation would be caused; 3. Many bankruptcies would be caused; 4. The levelling tendencies of the times would be fostered; 5. The utilitarian spirit of the age would be encouraged."* Well they were warned.

Former Ryde and Newport 2-4-0T No.5 around 1910, recalling the days when PRECURSOR had sallied back and forth during the opening day of the Cowes and Newport, 'hauling three carriages gaily bedecked with laurel and bunting' and the original Newport terminus was crowded with spectators. The new station after Swarbrick's intervention (see text) was put up some yards to the east in the 1870s, leaving only a couple of sidings to mark the site of the original terminus. Regarding the position of the new station there had (as we have seen) been much disagreement between the Ryde and Newport and the Cowes and Newport companies, the former wanting it further to the south at Coppins Bridge. In the period 1872/3 the proposed station was habitually labelled 'Coppins Bridge' in the minutes. Improved management kept the Central afloat, if not out of the water, through the 1880s and 1890s. Not only was a modest dividend paid, on more than one occasion, but new works were possible. The development of Medina Wharf was a bold step and the reconstruction and reorganisation of the early '90s – rebuilding Cowes station and confirming Newport as the engineering and commercial centre, showed further foresight. Before the close of the century the room available for financial manoeuvre had decreased sharply.

instead of by the Agency of the Isle of Wight Central Company, I think it desirable that you should be in possession of the whole of the facts relating to the change which has just taken place.

As you are aware, the Freshwater Line, which is about 12 miles long, was constructed by a junction with the former Newport & Cowes Railway, the junction pointing in the direction of Cowes, and not in the direction of the Newport Station, with the obvious intention of running trains between Cowes and Freshwater.

Sufficient land was purchased to provide a separate Station for Goods and Passengers, and running powers were given into Newport Station. A Working Agreement was entered into with the Isle of Wight Central Company, and renewed from time to time, but the Agreement did not provide for maintenance which was undertaken by the Freshwater Company.

Some two years ago a new Agreement was practically forced upon the Directors of the Freshwater Company, under which the Isle of Wight Central Company maintained the line up to a point, the proportion of receipts payable to the Freshwater Company being 25%. The maintenance Agreement was, however, so worded that it only provided for the upkeep of the Railway to enable trains to be run with safety, it did not cover ordinary wear and tear nor structural works, stations or buildings, and the Isle of Wight Central Company were to be at liberty to deal with all necessary works outside the pure upkeep of the roadbed and rails and to charge the Freshwater Company with the cost. The position forced upon the Directors clearly indicated that in a comparatively short time the line would fall into the hands of the Isle of Wight Central Company, and they (the Freshwater Company) were forced to make the necessary arrangements to work the Railway themselves.

Upon this being intimated to the Isle of Wight Central Company, the Chairman, at interviews with myself, stated that they should put in a Receiver, the Chairman having purchased £500 of 2nd Debenture Stock and the Deputy Chairman some £1,600 which Stock was, of course, purchased at a very low price, something between £15 and £20 per hundred, and they joining with three or four other Debenture Holders, who held altogether something like £2,000, commenced an action for judgement upon arrears of Debenture Interest, thus obliging the Directors, who represented the holders of some £180,000 Stock (of various classes including Debentures) out of a total of £225,000, the Company's Capital, to apply, much against their will, for Receivers and Managers in order to protect their property.

I, having advised the late Sir Blundell Maple some 16 years ago when he purchased nearly the whole of the Ordinary and Preference Stock, the whole of the 3rd Debenture, with the exception of £400, about three quarters of the second Debentures and 16,000 out of 20,000 of the 1st Debentures, the Directors asked me if I would join Mr F.G. Aman in the Receivership, to which I consented.

Newport station from the drawbridge on 4th August 1956. Disused Sandown line on left – Ryde line on right. Photograph A.E. Bennett.

The Southern Railway's wholesale renewal and updating of the island system manifested itself almost from the outset, judicious amendments at vital junctions, better locomotives and rolling stock and improved signalling. At Newport this included a renewal of the goods yard, situated on the site of the original Cowes and Newport Railway terminus, where four sidings replaced the earlier two. They are readily apparent in this view.

ALVERSTONE arriving at Newport from Cowes on a Sandown train. Another O2 waits in the Freshwater bay on the left. Further alterations at Newport included the extension of the northern end of the down platform (Nos. 1 & 2) thereby lengthening the Freshwater Bay and allowing the elimination of the old Freshwater Co. station, subject of so much fuss. This northernmost loco water tank (a 'balloon' or 'parachute' tank) was necessarily resited when the bay platform was increased in length to 245 feet. A coal stage was to be built on the far side, presumably for engines on Freshwater line workings but this particular detail of the scheme does not appear to have been carried out. Photograph S.W. Baker.

Waiting for trains. The canopies are thought to have been original but were of course altered somewhat over the years, in the normal course of repairs and maintenance. They were a standard design of Andrew Handyside, Derby. Newport was by a long measure the major junction station on the island and dealt with a considerable traffic, despite these somnolent views. Conacher was nothing if not sanguine: "...all I say is that anybody really conversant with railway problems will watch with much appreciative interest the skill with which the Cowes, Ryde, Freshwater and Sandown (or Ventnor) trains, when all meet in Newport Station – with its two through platforms and two docks – are handled and their passengers, etc., interchanged as required. It is done so well that nobody need desire anything better".

Newport in the 1930s. The *County Press* in January 1927 noted 'the station is now being reconstructed at a cost of £25,000.' A general renewal of the signalling had been approved in February 1909.

The Freshwater Bay at Newport. Trains off the Freshwater Yarmouth and Newport line set in here before 'The Dispute', recommencing when an agreement (the court heard the case over two days in February) was got together in 1914. Courtesy R. Randell.

View off the Freshwater line.

33 BEMBRIDGE on 4.35pm Ryde Pier to Cowes leaving Newport on 28th September 1951. 30 SHORWELL beyond. Collection John Scrace.

It was obvious that with the relationship existing between the two Companies it would not be practicable to continue to pay for the use of the Central Company's Station at Newport for which a large sum was demanded together with more siding accommodation for the transfer of from half a dozen trucks of goods per day, and further that the use of the Station would place in the hands of the Central Company, not only the train service, but the whole of the cash derived from Newport traffic, a very large proportion of the whole revenue, and to have continued running trains in and out of the Station would inevitably have placed the Company in such a position that ready cash would at certain times of the year have been too short to meet the current expenses, and they were therefore driven to build their own Station which has been done in the most convenient position, and as near as possible to the platforms of the Central Company, the distance between the two platforms being some 80 feet.

There need be no difficulty whatever in dealing with this miniature traffic if the Central Company were so minded. There is a certain amount of inconvenience at present and if the obstructive course is continued in it will prevent the Freshwater Company from doing as much as it could do for the public convenience.

It may be mentioned that the Central Company commenced an Action in the Commissioners' Court to compel the Freshwater Company to exchange traffic through the junction, but there has been no opposition whatever to the passage of traffic at the junction, and goods, mails, and mineral traffic is taken through daily in the same way as always has been done since the opening of the Railway, although no settlement has been arrived at for the proportion of receipts, and it is probable that some drastic action will have to be taken by the Receivers to obtain cash before conveyance for the prepaid traffic passing from the Central Railway.

The answer of the Freshwater Company to the Action before the Railway Commissioners led to a request by the Isle of Wight Central Company to postpone the hearing and they subsequently asked the master at the Court of Chancery for authority to proceed against the Receivers which authority was refused and I understand they are now proposing to ask the judge for such authority.

The whole object of the application is not to provide for transfer at the junction but to compel the Freshwater Company to make use of their Station which for reasons already indicated the Receivers cannot agree to do.

I may add that the Central Company endeavoured to get all the Authorities in the island, and a number of other people, to back up their application, but in every instance I am given to understand they met with a refusal.

It may be interesting to note also that the train service now given on the Freshwater line is more frequent and far more punctual than was the case when it was worked by the Isle of Wight Central company, and as a

31 CHALE on Cowes train; 17 SEAVIEW station pilot, 1964. Photograph T.P. Cooper.

Newport, looking towards Ryde, 21st April 1957. Photograph Derek Clayton.

At the south end of Newport station an iron footbridge was put up, described on 21st December 1889 as 'newly erected'. The corrugated iron covering was added subsequently, in Isle of Wight Central times, to be removed late in the BR period, around 1960.

BONCHURCH post–war backs out of Newport with the 9.43am Shanklin to Freshwater train, 13th September 1948. This was essentially the Southern 'Tourist'; Shanklin, later Ventnor (Sandown on Saturdays) via Merstone and reversing at Newport for the Freshwater line. Return from Freshwater was at about 6.00pm, with the stock used on ordinary services during the day. Collection John Scrace.

consequence the local traffic has very considerably improved.

Yours Truly,

Sam Fay.

The bridge over the Medina forms, in a sense, a convenient cut off to what might be termed the 'Cowes and Newport section' of the island's railways. Its operation, or rather the shortcomings thereof, were something of a sore point amongst Newport shipping interests, who were pressed eventually (in 1897) to take Court action. They lost but in the process it was reported, opening took 12 minutes, with two men on the winch. This must have been quite serious for the railway, for assuming a further twelve minutes for repositioning and only six minutes for a vessel's passing the main line was blocked half an hour for every ship. Some further work was presumably carried out in the 1890s, for on 2nd October 1895 the Directors were shown a letter from the Board of Trade 'stating that Colonel Addison would inspect the opening bridge at Newport'. The work may not have been unconnected with an incident of 1892:

"Last evening (14th October) an alarming accident occurred to a goods train on the IWCR whilst in the act of crossing the bridge which spans the Medina at Newport. It appears that at about 7.30 a goods train consisting of half a dozen trucks laden chiefly with coal, was leaving Newport station for Ryde when by some means or other the engine ran off the metals dragging several of the trucks off after it. It was impossible to stop the engine before it got onto the first span of the bridge and from the place where it left the rails it tore up the permanent way and splintered the woodwork of the bridge. Last night the engine was standing in an awkward position immediately over the river and her fore part had apparently sunk through the bridge considerably. The fact that some of the trucks were off the rails increased the embarrassment as they could not easily be shifted to their original position. Under the supervision of Mr. Simmons a large gang of workmen was speedily summoned to the scene of the accident and did their best to clear the line by the light of torches. The spectacle attracted a large number of spectators to the quay. Naturally the mishap blocked the Ryde line and passengers intending to travel by that train were promptly despatched to their destinations in cabs provided by the railway company."

From another correspondent:

".. the train consisted of six loaded trucks drawn by the engine 'Precursor'. One of the rails beyond the points and about 20 yards before the parapet of the bridge gave way, snapping about a yard from the end as the engine passed over it, although the rails were said to be 'proved steel'. The engine was naturally thrown onto the permanent way and proceeded about 40 feet before it could be stopped. The engine was now on the drawbridge and sank into the woodwork up to the level of the driving axles. Fortunately the engine, which weighs about 16 tons, was

35 FRESHWATER at Newport, about 1964, telegraph pole neatly sprouting from its chimney. Photograph T.P. Cooper.

Summer at Newport. Photograph T.P. Cooper.

24 CALBOURNE leaves Newport on the 2.35pm Ryde – Cowes, 21st August 1965. Photograph Leslie Sandler.

The water tank at Newport was an imposing structure, mounted improbably over one of the engine shed roads. It appears to have been an original feature, though £45 was put aside in 1911 for 'raising the loco water tank'. (This is doubtful since further references note different costs). Water was supplied by the Corporation at an annual cost by 1912 of about £180. They would not reduce the price of 7d per 1,000 gallons and the Central asked Messrs. Duke and Ockenden (or perhaps it was Messrs. Duke of Ockenden – the minutes are often muddled) to sink a bore, cost £300, on the company's property. 'If successful it is intended that a pump be purchased making the annual cost only £60. Raising the existing tank would cost £25.' In May 1913 the bore had penetrated without success to 175 feet but 'abundant water ... was reached at 560 feet. The company hope to get a supply in a few weeks once an electric motor has been bought.' The cost by now had risen to £900. The engine shed had been built in timber planking on a wooden frame but was refitted in corrugated sheeting, beloved of the Southern.

over one of the massive longitudinal girders which run under the rails and this alone prevented it from being precipitated into the river. Five trucks left the rails with the engine. Happily the engineer and manager were in the vicinity at the time and immediately took active measures to clear the line, not only in putting on a strong gang of platelayers with fitters from the works but despatching spare engines to collect all available hands from other portions of the line. The men worked with a will and soon had three trucks back on the metals and run out of the way. The two trucks next to the engine, which were further off the metals, were speedily unloaded, the gravel they contained being thrown over the parapet of the bridge with the Little London roadway below. This facilitated their replacement on the rail."

There was a further mishap on the bridge in 1896, embarrassing and amusing in retrospect but potentially lethal:

"During Monday night a railway coal truck which had been discharging in the neighbourhood of the Quay railway bridge was pushed on to make room for another. Apparently not having the brake on sufficiently hard the truck ran onto the bridge which had been left open for the passage of vessels during the night and was precipitated into the river with an alarming splash. Fortunately the passage was clear underneath and the damage was confined to the truck."

In November 1890 the tender of T. Jenkins (a Newport builder) had been approved 'for the erection of two Locomotive Sheds at Newport'. £1,798.10s had been accepted and 'Contract and Specification for same were sealed'. Purchase of the necessary land from Winchester College was not finally complete however until December and 'Engines were moved to Newport from Cowes on 2nd February 1891.' Confusion arises over the wording of the Contract – it probably refers to the shed and the works though three main buildings were put up at Newport; works, engine shed and a two road through structure opposite the north signal box. This, from plans, appears little more than a canopy and in all probability served relatively briefly as carriage shed. In October 1903 permission was given to 'remove the carriage shed'. The bright modern shed alongside was the new BR staff block, a system of building developed on the Southern.

Newport engine shed in early British Railways days. From the first locos were based on Cowes, presumably returning thence at night. The joint station of 1875, with workings on the Ryde and Newport to Ryde, the Sandown trains etc., rendered Cowes awkward as a locomotive base. It must very soon have been apparent that a pit at least was required at Newport for locomotives of the other two companies. What provision was made (if any) is unknown, however. The formal amalgamation of the companies into the Isle of Wight Central resulted almost immediately in moves to establish new premises at Newport. Application was made to the Council in December of 1887 to move 'the works' from Cowes, one outcome of which would be the removal of a siding down to the quay. The following February an offer was received from the Isle of Wight Railway as to joint use of their shops at Ryde. This was 'favourably entertained' but nothing further is recorded beyond a decision 'to ask for definite terms'. 1,000 tons of steam coal was ordered on 30th October 1889 'at Newport 12s 6d per ton less 2½% for cash'. At the beginning of 1895 one J. Seymour was appointed Locomotive Foreman, initially for three years at a salary of £3 per week 'inclusive of 10s in the second year and a further 10s in the third year'.

CALBOURNE again (it seems to figure a lot in these pages – by pure chance), fresh ex–works and on the Newport station pilot duty. 2nd June 1965. Photograph T.P. Cooper.

Left. Newport shed, 22nd September 1956, ASHEY and WHITWELL, with YARMOUTH beyond, dead in the yard. In January 1902 Conacher obtained estimates for tarring and repairing 'the large workshop and the Engine Running Shed.' Jenkins, the original builder, successfully tendered for the latter at £78, whilst Barton & Co. got the bigger job, at £150. The Central equipped the works with secondhand machinery bought cheap from mainland companies. The original shear legs for loco lifting seem to have been located at the works, and were replaced in 1939. The old set was in bad condition and when in use blocked the carriage repair shop anyway! In 1905 Conacher successfully recommended to the Board that Newport works be closed for a week that Christmas 'to reduce expenses', though how this was done and whether it became an annual event is not clear. It was a poor Yule if it were wages that were to be saved. Photograph S.W. Baker.

There were four E1 0–6–0Ts on the island in the 1950s; this is No.2 YARMOUTH, parked at the side of Newport shed on 26th June 1955. Photograph A.E. Bennett.

This is where we can consider the Cowes and Newport to end, the bridge over the Medina at the southern end of Newport station. Beyond it lay the rest of the island lines, exotic places (Cowes to Newport was after all more or less a relative backwater) such as Ventnor, Shanklin, Ryde and the rest. *Multum in Parvo!*. Photograph Derek Clayton.

No.2 YARMOUTH again, on 7th July 1955, under the crude canopy associated with the coaling stage. Photograph P.J. Kelley.

Approaching Newport from Sandown in the summer of 1953, high above the cluttered buildings (low gabled in island fashion) and mill ponds of the Medina. It was a shabby area, a peculiarly industrial setting possessing nevertheless great charm. There were unfortunately few regrets when the whole unlovely lot was bulldozed, principally it would appear, in order to accommodate a roundabout of painful neatness. Today it is almost impossible to imagine that a railway junction, of singular interest and history, had ever been here. Photograph H.C. Casserley.

ENDPIECE

A last peep through the the cab of BEMBRIDGE, by A.E. Bennett in 1955, and a suitable note on which to end this look at the Cowes and Newport line. It has proved, I hope, both illuminating and, perhaps more importantly, amusing. The island is vastly catered for with respect to its railway history, far beyond what might be expected, given its modest size. Readers can avail themselves of any number of publications for chapter and verse on all sorts of technical aspects – locos, rolling stock, their dates and dimensions, and the voodoo world of workings and timetables; in the account above I have attempted, in a slim volume, something at least of the background to one island line and its evolution, in terms of people and places, and bricks and mortar. If it's found to be a bit idiosyncratic in parts I'll be pleased; I believe a fair bit of the story is seeing print for the first time, so if it adds a little at least to the Eden Isle's store of railway lore, then I'll be happy too.

This look at the Cowes and Newport has been almost painfully long in the making; this is the second publisher to have it in their possession and it has suffered unlooked–for disasters at least twice, when press dates were at last in sight. It has been a hard slog, no place for fainthearts, to be sure, and so it is with the greatest pleasure that I thank those whose long–standing help has succoured the book. Much of the nitty gritty of the local story, as well as the photographic content, owes an enormous amount to Tim Cooper. I wish also to thank George Reeve, John Hooper, Wendy Smith and Chris Hawkins, Graham Smith – and the formidable Sheila. Especial thanks also to Reg Randell, who doubtless has long given up hope of seeing the thing.